DATE DUE

Caves for Kids
in Historic New York

Caves for Kids
in Historic New York

PATRICIA EDWARDS CLYNE
illustrated with maps and photographs

Library Research Associates
Monroe, N.Y. 1980

OTHER BOOKS BY THE AUTHOR

The Corduroy Road

Tunnels of Terror

Patriots in Petticoats

Ghostly Animals of America

Patricia Edwards Clyne
Copyright ©1980

Printed in the United States of America.

14930

ISBN 0-912526-24-6

Clyne, Patricia Edwards.
 Caves for kids in historic New York

 Bibliography: p.
 SUMMARY: A guide to exploring 19 caves in New York, including historical information about the caverns and notes on caving.
 1. Caves—New York (State) [1. Caves—New York (State)] I. Title.
GV200.655.N7C58   796.5'25'09747   78-31634

 [During the months that have elapsed between the time the author last visited the caves described and the publication of this book, it is possible for conditions to have changed at some of the sites. Hence, readers are advised to check ahead before visiting any of these locations.]

Maps by WASYL BANYCKYJ

Dedicated

to

My partner in cave-hunting

as well as in life,

my husband Frank,

and to

Nicholas Shoumatoff,

who first "introduced" me

to the Old Leatherman

I find there is enough of
the troglodyte in most
persons to make them love
the rocks and the caves and
ledges that the air and the
rains have carved out of them.

—John Burroughs
Under the Apple-Trees

Contents

Introduction

There is something especially fascinating about a cave. Whether it be a limestone room carved out by an underground stream or the result of giant boulders piled up by some long-ago glacier, there is always a sense of strangeness, of adventure and of history.

It was a cave that served as man's first permanent home, and because of this scientists have learned many things by exploring caves. But ancient man was not the only one who enjoyed the shelter these "natural homes" afforded. Down through the ages, men have continued to use them, usually as a home, or for storage, often as a hideout, and sometimes as a shelter for animals.

The State of New York is punctured by hundreds of caves and one of them is the largest in the Northeast. This is Howe Caverns which, because of its underground river and countless rooms of unusual geological formations, has become world-famous.

But no matter how beautiful such a giant cavern may be, it was more often the small caves — sometimes merely rock shelters — that man chose to live in. The reason was not only that small caves were more plentiful, but they were easier to heat and they were safer. For only in a small cave could a man see before entering whether any predatory animal or other enemy was lurking inside.

Just as these smaller caves were chosen for safety by the people who once inhabited them, the ones included in this book have been chosen for the safety of those young people who have a yen to go cave exploring.

Another reason for selecting these caves is that all of them have interesting histories. *Caves For Kids* is not intended to be a textbook, however, and each chapter begins with a fictionalized story based on the known facts concerning the cave and whoever was associated with it.

Among them you will discover the rock homes of the Wickquaskeek Indians, who fought Henry Hudson when he explored the river which now bears his name. Farther to the northeast is the cave which sheltered the religious liberal Anne Hutchinson as she made her way from Rhode Island to what is now Eastchester, New York. Then there are the various caves of a gentle but mysterious wanderer called the Old Leatherman.

A cave also served as a haven for the "cowboy" Claudius Smith, who terrorized the New York-New Jersey border, while another was used for a bloody ambush during the late 1700's. At least two caves provided inspiration for novelist James Fenimore Cooper, and the year-round coolness of a deep cleft served as an icebox for naturalist John Burroughs.

You may think that hermits have always been men, but this is not so, as you will discover when you visit the rock shelter of Sarah Bishop. She chose a solitary mountain home with a view of Long Island, where she had been born.

There is even a cave which served as a "factory" for counterfeit money, as well as one which was a hideout for two lovers running away from servitude under Napoleon Bonaparte's niece. Still another provided safety for the Pequot Indian chief Sassacus after his tribe was defeated in Connecticut.

These are only some of New York's historic *Caves For Kids,* all of which are accessible to the general public, and safe enough for even the most inexperienced adventurer. They are just as nature made them, which, most people agree, enhances the fun of exploring them on your own. As for finding them, photographs, map sketches and detailed directions have been provided at the end of each chapter.

None of these caves is commercially operated. Therefore, there are no admission charges. In addition, most of them are located in state or county parks — an added advantage if you visit them in a large group.

But even if you only plan to explore them through the pages of this story book/guide book, you will find each offers a tale that will take you back to another time and to the people who contributed to the rich history of New York State.

Caves for Kids
in Historic New York

1 The Indians of Inwood

It was corn harvest time in the village near the salt marsh. For many days now the women of the Wickquaskeek tribe had labored in the hot sun of late summer. They were pulling the last beans from the vines that had entwined themselves around the sturdy cornstalks.

Corn Flower well knew that the hardest work was yet to come. As she raised an earthenware jar in her arms, the Indian girl thought of the long weeks ahead when the fat ears of corn would be broken off. Most of them would be stored for winter in the pits on the side of the hill. New pits had to be dug because, as previously stored food was used and the pits were emptied, they were filled with discarded shells of oysters, which were a favorite tribal food.

From storage pit to garbage pit—so many shells for such a small amount of oyster meat. Corn Flower sighed as she walked toward the spring on the salt marsh. She would think about digging the new pits tomorrow. Right now there was water to be hauled back to the cave where her mother was waiting.

Corn Flower knelt by the gushing spring and filled the pottery jar. Then rising, she stood there a moment longer and looked out across the sparkling waters beyond the salt marsh. Perhaps her brother Beaver Claw would be returning from his day's fishing.

She squinted her dark eyes against the glare of the

3

sun on the water. Then, Corn Flower gasped in fear. The earthenware jar slipped from her arms and fell to the soft earth without breaking. Water splashed all over her moc-casined feet, but the Indian girl was unaware of this as she stared at the huge thing sailing toward the salt marsh where she stood.

"Ai-yee! It is a sea monster!"

The scream ripped through the afternoon air, startling Corn Flower out of her state of shocked immobili-ty. Spinning around, she saw an old woman from the village.

"A giant fish! A sea monster!" the woman screamed again. Then the old woman darted up the trail to the vil-lage, with Corn Flower right behind.

Within minutes the men of the village had assem-bled along the edge of the salt marsh. With narrowed eyes, they studied the frightening thing coming toward them. It seemed to have giant quills sticking out from its back like some monstrous seagoing porcupine.

High on the hill above the salt marsh, Corn Flower trembled as she watched. Her mother had wanted her to stay in the safety of their cave home, but Beaver Claw was now down there with the men, and Corn Flower had to see what happened. In any event, the sea monster was no longer moving. It had stayed in the same place, bobbing up and down in the water, ever since the men of the village had raced down to the salt marsh.

Suddenly a murmuring broke the silence. It grew in volume as the men started chattering among them-selves. Some even laughed as they excitedly pointed toward the water.

It was no sea monster, after all. It was just some sort of huge canoe filled with men. These men had lowered a smaller canoe into the water and some of them were now heading for the shore.

As they came closer, the Wickquaskeeks could see the white skin of the strangers. But even with white skin, these were men just as they were.

They had heard stories about men with pale skins

that had come to trade with other villages. But they had thought these were only stories—the kind of wild tales that were told around the fire during the long winter nights. Now they could see for themselves that there really were such white-faced men.

With cheerful cries, the men directed the women to prepare goods for trading—wild grapes, tobacco and furs—with these strangers. Meanwhile, some of them paddled out to see the giant canoe with the quills that stood up in the air like those of a startled porcupine.

The festive air did not last long, however. For when one of the canoes reached the anchored ship, the crew captured two of the Wickquaskeeks. Perhaps this was done as insurance against attack, or maybe they merely wanted two "specimens" to take back home with them. Whatever the reason, the two Indians wanted no part of it, and it was not long until they escaped.

One drowned in the rushing waters of what is now known as Spuyten Duyvil, the channel linking the Harlem and Hudson Rivers. The other Indian made his way to the village of Nipinisicken on the mainland, where a war council was soon under way. But immediately after the escape, the ship had slipped anchor and was well on its way up the river by the time the lone survivor reached the village.

Aboard the *Half Moon,* its Dutch captain, Henry Hudson, was intent on exploring the river in the hope of finding a route to China. Therefore, he probably thought no more of the incident. But the Wickquaskeeks would not forget—and their lives would never be the same after that fateful September day.

The harvest was still in progress when Henry Hudson returned from his journey up the river. His ship anchored near the village of the caves on October 2, 1609. The angry Wickquaskeeks did not stand in awe this time. Instead, they promptly launched two canoes to attack the *Half Moon.* Their bows and arrows were of little use against the ship's cannon, and after two of their men were killed, the Wickquaskeeks retreated.

A third canoe set out, but cannon and musket fire soon killed five of the party, and it, too, returned to shore. Helpless against the thundering fire of the invaders, the Wickquaskeeks fled into the dense woods, fearful that the white strangers would attack.

Henry Hudson was finished with them, however. With the *Half Moon* loaded with New World goods that he had bartered for from other Indians, he left the waters of Spuyten Duyvil to sail down the river that would eventually bear his name.

The Wickquaskeeks returned to their caves on the side of what is now called Cock's Hill in Inwood Park at the northern end of Manhattan Island. There they were to live in peace, except for occasional forays with neighboring tribes, until 1621, when the Dutch West India Company established trading colonies at Fort Orange (Albany) and Fort Amsterdam (New York).

It was near the gushing stream where Corn Flower first sighted the *Half Moon* that Peter Minuit bought the island of Manhattan for a reputed $24 worth of trade goods. (A bronze plaque on a rock now marks the spot.) However, the Wickquaskeeks did not seem to think this included their fertile valley (now called the Clove) at the foot of their caves, so they remained there—but not in peace.

Bloody attacks and reprisals by both white men and Indians marked the intervening years until 1715, when the Wickquaskeeks finally were forced to give up their cave homes.

The farmers took over and made an orchard of the Indians' corn and bean fields. And 175 years of spring rainfalls washed dirt and debris into the caves where Corn Flower and her people once lived. It would seem the Wickquaskeeks had been forgotten.

Years passed until 1890, when Alexander Chenoweth first discovered evidence of the ancient village in a dry stream bed at the bottom of Cock's Hill. Gazing upward at the overhanging rocks, he set out to explore them. Soon he came to a small opening in the tumbled boulders. Digging away years of accumulated soil, he found fragments of pottery and tools.

Inwood Hill Park

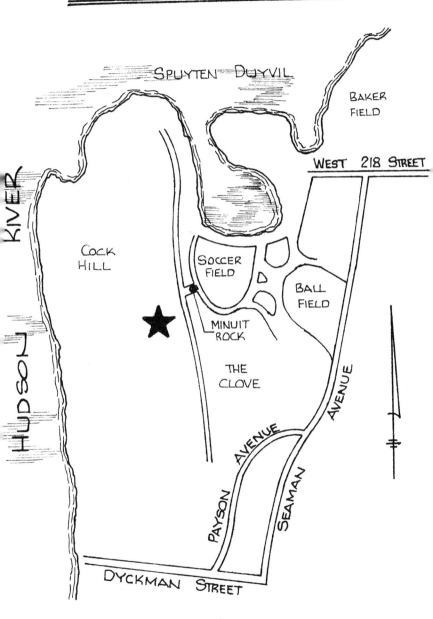

Convinced now of an important archeological find, Chenoweth and some friends soon excavated the cave. They discovered that it led to a second, larger chamber containing a primitive fireplace. In time, two other caves were uncovered, along with numerous artifacts now housed in the American Museum of Natural History.

Although no artifacts have been found there in recent years, the Indian Caves of Inwood remain an intriguing spot for exploration—and a memorial to a peace-loving people who lived there long before the mighty Hudson River had a name.

How to Get There

Inwood Caves, Inwood Park, New York, New York. The quickest and easiest way to reach the caves is to enter the northern end of Inwood Park at West 218 Street. Head west, going past Baker Field. Continue on the concrete path that skirts the boat basin. (To your right, across the waters of Spuyten Duyvil, you will see a large blue "C"—for Columbia University—painted on the rock face. Just north of there was the village of Nipinisicken, where the war council was held.) Take the path around the soccer field (which used to be the salt marsh) to its southern end, where it circles to join another path leading south between two hills. This area is called the Clove. (At the point where the two paths join can be found the stone marker commemorating the purchase of Manhattan Island by Peter Minuit.)

Continue south down this path a few hundred feet, until you come to the caves which you will see above you on your right. Several footpaths lead up to them from the main path. (Approximate walking time: 10 minutes from West 218 Street entrance.)

2 Haven for Anne Hutchinson

Never had they seen a night so dark, and their fear made it seem even darker. Around sunset, heavy clouds had begun to blanket the sky, so that now no moon or stars relieved the ebony blackness outside the mouth of the cave.

They had hoped to come across a farmhouse, for they were nearing exhaustion from their long trek from Aquidneck Island. But one of the horses had strayed off during their midday rest, and they were forced to spend more than an hour looking for it.

"We were fortunate to find this cave," Anne Hutchinson said suddenly, as if reading the mind of her youngest son, Zuriel.

The other five children looked up at the sound of their mother's voice, making six pairs of blue eyes which stared at her across the tiny fire.

For a brief moment, Anne almost gave way to her fear, and she fervently wished that her husband could be there to help them. But William was dead, and they had only themselves to rely on to get to their new home north of New Amsterdam.

"Yes, we are fortunate," Anne repeated. "At least here in this cave we can enjoy a fire that the Indians will

not see. With the blanket across the cave's mouth, we are safe and secure."

If her voice had quavered over the last words, she hoped her children did not notice it. She was certain they were not aware of what she had found on the ledge above the cave entrance when they first arrived. Seeking a spot from which to hang the blanket to cover the mouth of the cave, Anne had climbed up on the ledge. There, in the fading light of the cloud-covered sunset, she had seen signs that others had used this cave before them. But those others ran on four legs and possessed claws and fangs.

While her sons had been unloading their baggage from the horses, the stalwart woman had tossed stones into the dark recesses of the cave, hoping to flush out any predator that lingered there. But the bobcats—or whatever had made the tracks on the ledge—were no longer there, and Anne had seen no reason to mention them to her family.

Nor did she mention what she had discovered only a short while ago when they were eating their meager supper. A small gust of wind had rushed through some hidden crevice in the cave. It caused the small fire to flare up brightly for only a few moments. But in that time Anne's quick eyes had spotted a circle of stones on the other side of the cave and a smoke-blackened wall above.

Yes, there had been others here before them—human as well as animal. She could only pray that whoever had constructed that rude fireplace would not return this night.

Looking over at her youngest son, she found him studying her. "What are you doing with that stick?" she asked in an attempt to divert the question he seemed about to ask.

The stick dropped from his fingers as if she had caught him doing something he shouldn't. Then with a nervous laugh, Zuriel explained, "Just figuring out how far we have come."

A long, long way, Anne wanted to say, but instead she pointed to the others who were now asleep, huddled

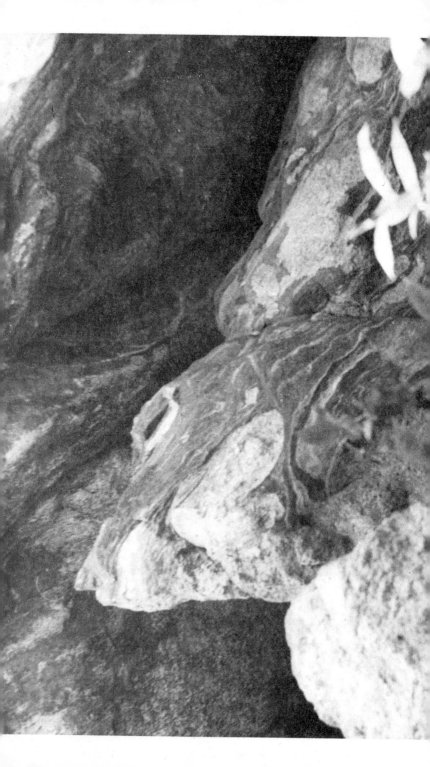

near the sputtering flames of the dying fire. "We'd best be joining them," she said. "For we have many miles to cover on the morrow."

But Anne Hutchinson did not sleep much that night. From time to time she would add a few sticks to the fire. The words of her son kept her awake as much as her anxiety over their safety.

How far, indeed, had she come? The first journey had been all the way from England to Massachusetts. She might have stayed there, too, had it not been for her disagreement with the Puritans who ruled the colony.

Everything had been alright when Sir Harry Vane was governor. He had tolerated—even agreed with—her more liberal religious views, and she had been allowed to hold prayer meetings in her home. There were many people, even ministers, who came there to hear her views on Christianity, some of which were in direct conflict with the rigid Puritan beliefs.

Then Governor Vane had been replaced by John Winthrop, who not only disagreed with Anne's views, but also her right to express them in public. It was not long thereafter that she was tried in public court, excommunicated from the church and then banished from Massachusetts Colony.

Undaunted, Anne and her husband William had gathered their followers and established a settlement in Aquidneck Island (later called Rhode Island). But then this year, 1642, her husband had died and Anne had decided to move farther south.

So it was that she had come a long, long way, and there was still much ground to cover before they reached what Anne hoped would be their permanent home.

The heavy cloud layer that had obscured the moon and stars was still present the next morning when Anne awoke to see the first grayish light that passed for dawn. Working quickly, she had everything ready for their departure as soon as the others woke up and had something to eat.

While waiting for them to finish, Anne idly picked

up the stick her son had been using the night before. But where Zuriel supposedly had been figuring the miles they had traveled, there was only a shallow hole in the dirt floor of the cave.

Puzzled, she took his arm as they were leaving the cave, and pointed back to the small hole now visible in the rays of light penetrating the cave.

Without speaking, Zuriel put his hand into his pocket and withdrew several pieces of what first appeared to be rock. Closer inspection proved they were rock alright, but rock that had been carefully chipped at and fashioned into sharp points.

"Arrowheads!" Anne gasped.

Holding his fingers to his lips, her son pointed to his sisters and brother already outside the cave. "I didn't want to alarm them," he explained, "or for you to worry through the night."

Smiling with motherly pride, Anne Hutchinson took Zuriel's hand in hers. For a moment she was tempted to tell him of her own discoveries in the cave. But then she decided against it. He had tried to protect her from worry, and she did not want to make less of this gift of love he had given her. Therefore, all she said was a simple "Thank you" as she left the cave to resume their journey to a new life.

The Hutchinson family traveled southeast to a point near what is now called Pelham Bay, New York, not far from the town of Eastchester. There they remained for a year until, one day, the very thing Anne had feared in the cave happened. Rampaging Indians attacked their home, massacring Anne and her children, except for eight-year-old Susanna Hutchinson, who was taken into captivity, but later ransomed.

The cave where Anne Hutchinson stayed was, indeed, an Indian refuge. Many years later archeologists were to discover a large number of arrowheads and other artifacts there.

Though Anne Hutchinson was its most famous tenant, the cave was named for another later inhabitant,

HELICKER'S CAVE

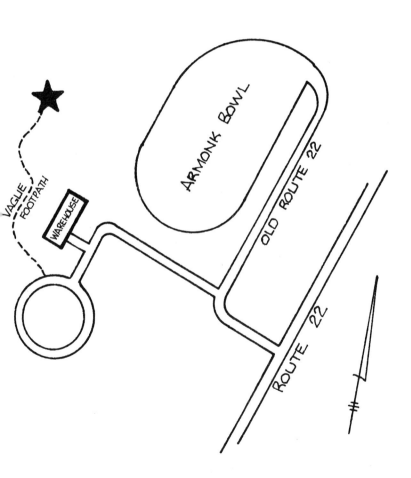

who moved in some time after the Revolutionary War ended. From about 1783 to 1802, a hermit known as Old Bet
Helicker lived there. When he died, the cave lay abandoned until after the Civil War when it was used
periodically by a mysterious wanderer called the Old
Leatherman. But that is another story told elsewhere in
this book.

How to Get There

Helicker's Cave, west of Route 22, Armonk, New York.
Just south of the main business district of Armonk, there
is an exit west off Route 22, leading to Old Route 22.
Take this exit and bear left down the incline to the indus-
trial area at the foot of the hill. (In wet weather be certain
to wear rubber boots, as the ground is swampy at the base
of the hill.) You will see a warehouse. Directly in back of
the northwestern corner of the warehouse, about a third of
the way up the hill, you will see a ledge of grayish-white
rocks. Beneath this is Helicker's Cave. A vague footpath
leads up to the cave. (Approximate walking time: 10
minutes from Old Route 22.)

3 Lairs of the Leatherman

Jeremy stood panting in the heat of the July sun. He was waiting for the words of praise that would surely come from Aunt Esther's lips. But the tiny woman only stood on the porch staring down at the boy. Then suddenly three words seared through the air:

"You did what?"

Unsure of himself now, the boy stammered, "I . . . I was up near that . . . that cave on the ridge. Somebody's been using it to live in. There were sticks and cans and firewood all over. I know Uncle Josh doesn't like squatters or tramps on his property, so I . . ."

"You had no right to touch the Leatherman's things!" the woman interrupted, her tone more urgent than angry. "Now you go right back up there and replace everything just the way you found it." She paused a moment for breath, then added, "Else he might never come back!"

"But Aunt Esther, I . . ."

"Hurry now — the Leatherman's due through here any day."

The confused and tired boy could only nod obediently. Then he turned toward the high ridge from where he'd just come. It was a long walk back, and it would take at least an hour to find and replace all the things he'd

17

thrown out of the cave. But he didn't want Aunt Esther to be mad at him. After all, she and Uncle Josh had been nice enough to invite him to stay with them for the summer, instead of remaining in the humid heat of the city.

As Jeremy trudged back over the meadow returning to the small farmhouse, the sun was touching the blue-green spires of the hemlock forest to the west. His aunt saw him coming, and by the time the boy had reached the wide porch she was standing there with a glass of cool buttermilk in her hand.

"I'm sorry to have been so short with you, Jeremy," she began, "but you see, the Leatherman is...well...he's important to us all. Maybe when you've been here awhile, when you get to know about him, you'll understand."

Two days later, Jeremy did begin to understand. As he was helping his Uncle Josh fix the pump in the back yard, they heard an odd creaking sound coming from down the road.

Uncle Josh listened for a moment. Then a smile creased his weathered face. "That's him — right on schedule too." Turning to the house, he called, "The Leatherman's here, Esther."

Just as Aunt Esther hurried out the back door, Jeremy felt his breath catch in his throat. The creaking sound was louder now. There, trudging slowly over the rise in the dirt road, came the strangest looking man the boy had ever seen.

The man's clothes were made up of large pieces of leather crudely stitched together by thongs of the same material. The creaking sound was made by this ungainly outfit. A large sack, also of leather, was slung over his back, while his leather cap was pulled down over his eyes to shade them from the afternoon sun.

Without a word or gesture of greeting, the stocky figure walked past them to the wood lot, where he sat down heavily on a sawed-off tree stump. Within minutes, Aunt Esther was by his side, a pot of coffee in one hand, a bowl of stew in the other.

For several minutes the Leatherman gazed at the bowl of stew, obviously savoring the aroma. Then with a sad shake of his head, he reached for the chunk of bread Aunt Esther had set down next to the coffeepot.

Breaking up the bread into tiny chunks which he put into the saucer of coffee Aunt Esther had poured, the strange man proceeded to search in his satchel for a square piece of leather.

It was only then that Jeremy noticed the painful-looking sore on the man's lower lip. Using the piece of leather as a shield to protect the sore, he raised the saucer of coffee and now-soft bread to his mouth.

Astonished, Jeremy turned to his Aunt Esther for an explanation. Tears welled up in her blue eyes as she

whispered, "Poor man isn't even able to chew things anymore 'cause of the cancer on his lip."

Finished with his meal, the leather-clad man got up slowly, as if with great effort. Then picking up his satchel once more, he began to leave.

Just as he came abreast of Jeremy, Uncle Josh spoke up, "Please let us help you. At least stay the night. In the morning I can get a doctor who will. . ."

The bowed head was lifted, and the large, dark-blue eyes glanced at the farmer for just a second. They were the saddest eyes the boy had ever seen, yet there was kindness and gentleness in them too. Then without a word the Leatherman trudged away, his suit creaking, the satchel on his shoulder like some huge bundle of woe.

"No one knows where he came from," Uncle Josh told Jeremy later that night as they sat on the porch after supper. "And for a long time no one knew where he went. We don't even know for sure what his real name is."

Bedtime came and went, and still they sat on the porch as Uncle Josh told his nephew the story of their mysterious visitor. As he listened, Jeremy realized why his aunt had sent him back to the cave—and before he went to bed that night, the boy was very glad that she had.

It was in 1858 that the Leatherman first appeared, but not until almost three decades later did people begin to realize he traveled a specific route. He walked more than 300 miles every 34 days, from the Connecticut River southeast through New York's Westchester and Putnam Counties, then back again, winter and summer, year after lonely year.

At night he slept in one of the more than thirty caves he had discovered along his route, while during the day he would stop at a farmhouse for food. He rarely spoke, which at first prompted people to think he was mute. Later it was learned he could speak a kind of broken English.

When he first appeared, the Leatherman was looked on with fear, and most people fed him more from a

desire to get rid of him than any concern for his well-being. However, as the years passed and the odd figure in the creaking leather suit became a familiar sight, housewives began looking forward to his visits. They even vied with each other by cooking certain dishes on the day he was expected. In the loneliness of rural living, the Leatherman was a welcome diversion — an intriguing, walking mystery.

Who was he? Why had he chosen such a regular route — almost as if it was something he *had* to do? And why did he wear that ungainly leather costume when he was constantly being offered better and more comfortable clothing? No one knew, for the Leatherman would not speak.

Finally in 1885, the *Hartford Globe* published a detailed account of the Leatherman's route, and his tragic story was finally made public.

Although there are different versions of the story, it is generally accepted that the Leatherman's real name was Jules Bourglay and that he was born in Lyons, France. As a young man he fell in love with the daughter of a wealthy leather merchant named Laron. But Jules had neither wealth nor position, and the merchant frowned on any alliance between the two.

Had his daughter not been so enamored with the young man, Laron might have abruptly broken the romance. However, bending to his daughter's entreaties, he agreed — under certain conditions — to take Jules into the leather business. If, within a year, Jules proved successful, Laron would give his blessing to their marriage. On the other hand, if the young man did not prove his worth, he was to give up all claim to the daughter and leave the vicinity.

Jules readily agreed to honor Laron's terms and was placed in a responsible position in the merchant's leather business. However, speculation, inexperience and one of the severest depressions in the leather market were three factors neither young Jules nor Laron had reckoned with Before the year was up, Jules was directly respon-

sible for a financial disaster that ended any hope he might have of marrying the girl he loved.

Some accounts say that the daughter was subsequently killed in a mysterious fire that destroyed the merchant's home. Other stories relate only that young Jules became insane with grief and spent several years in an asylum before coming to the United States. But most of them agree that his lonely route was a sort of sorrowful lament — or penance — for a lost love, and the leather suit a symbol of his failure.

Needless to say, an already active interest in the Leatherman was heightened by such accounts. This was added to when newspapers reported that a young man had discovered the Leatherman lying ill in a cave near Woodbury, Connecticut. While nursing the Leatherman, the young fellow discovered he wore a crucifix around his neck and carried a French prayerbook published in 1844. Surely, this was proof that he was, indeed, Jules Bourglay. But the Leatherman said nothing.

Whether or not he was aware of the publicity concerning him is not known. In any event, he never varied his habits — even when it was obvious he was ill and in desperate need of medical care.

By 1888, when Jeremy first saw him, it was taking him longer to complete his circuit, and people began noticing an open sore on his lip that gradually spread. The pain must have been great even then, for he once allowed a doctor in Saybrook, Connecticut, to treat it and accepted some ointment before resuming his daily trek.

The sore grew worse during the ensuing months, but the Leatherman would not interrupt his travel until he was forced to do so on December 2, 1888. On that day, a committee initiated by the Connecticut Humane Society intercepted the Leatherman. He was taken to Hartford Hospital for treatment of the sore, which by now was eating away his lower jaw. However, since he had been specifically exempted from the Connecticut anti-tramp law, and since no other law covered such circumstances, there was no way the Leatherman could be forced to stay in the hospital.

Therefore, after being treated—for which he seemed thankful—the Leatherman was again on his solitary way, much to the consternation of the men who sought to help him.

He had less than four months to live.

His steps were slower now, almost stumbling at times, and he was forced to sit down and rest every few minutes. Yet still he went on until March 24, 1889. On that day his body was found sprawled face down in a rock shelter in Briarcliff, New York.

Since there had been rumors that he might have a fortune hidden in one of his shelters, and stories were told of a suspicious wound found in the back of his head, many people voiced the opinion that the Leatherman had been murdered.

The idea of a fortune had come about from newspaper stories that a man named Jules Martins had arrived from France in search of Jules Bourglay—otherwise known as the Leatherman—who had an inheritance awaiting him in his native land. Supposedly the two men were scheduled to meet near Bridgeport, Connecticut.

Whether the two men ever met, or whether there ever was a Jules Martins who came from France remains a mystery. But it is a mystery which resulted in fortune-hunters descending on all the then-known shelters used by the Leatherman.

No treasure was ever reported found. And, at an inquest held to determine the cause of the Leatherman's death, murder was ruled out. The jury concluded he had died of blood poisoning from the cancer which had reduced his once stocky body to an emaciated 140 pounds. He was estimated to have been about 55 to 65 years old.

Still the rumors persisted. Supposedly one of the Leatherman's packs was missing. There was even a report of the Leatherman's ghost seen near one of his caves.

In time, the wild rumors and tall tales became only whispers lost on the wind. But the story of the Leatherman would never die. There were too many people who had known him and continued to be intrigued by his mysterious and solitary ways.

Down through the years, there have been several books which told his story, and numerous articles have appeared in magazines and newspapers. Researchers even sought information on him as far away as France.

For the Leatherman's continuing popularity lies in the fact that he represents different things to different people. Some see only the tragedy of a lost love. Others marvel at his superior woodsmanship which allowed him to survive three decades of living in the open with only the most primitive equipment. Still others see in him a kind of total freedom—a freedom seemingly unobtainable in our modern society. For many he is symbolic of absolute loneliness, and there are those who are fascinated solely by the enigma he presents.

But whatever his image and whatever his name, it cannot be denied that the Old Leatherman has taken a

permanent place in the folklore of New York — and the
history of man.

How to Get There

Of the many Leatherman caves still in existence,
the following three have been chosen because of their ac-
cessibility and appearance.

*Leatherman's Cave, Ward Pound Ridge Reservation,
Cross River, New York.* (A map is available at the Trailside
Museum on Boutonville Road within the reservation.) At
the entrance to the park, a few feet past the toll booth,
turn right on School House Road and go south to where
School House Road merges with Honey Hollow Road.
Continue south until you see on the left side of the road a
chain barrier erected across a path leading east. The trail
is marked by three yellow dots and there is a sign posted
prohibiting snowmobiles from entering.

Follow this trail east, across a small wooden foot-
bridge, until you reach an opening in the rock wall to your
left (north). A path marked by three blue circles leads up
the hill from the stone fence. The cave is about 100 yards
up the trail and can easily be seen to your right as you approach it. (Approximate walking time: 10 minutes from
beginning of trail at Honey Hollow Road.)

Bull's Hill Cave, Bedford Hills, New York. Just west of
the Saw Mill River Parkway at the Bedford Hills exit, the
Bull's Hill Cave of the Leatherman can readily be spotted
from the highway (to your left going north), except in the
summer months when heavy vegetation masks its entrance. It is a steep climb (about 200 feet) up a narrow
path which is located at the northern end of a gas station.
But the spectacular view from the narrow ledge in front of

LEATHERMAN'S CAVE

BULL'S HILL CAVE

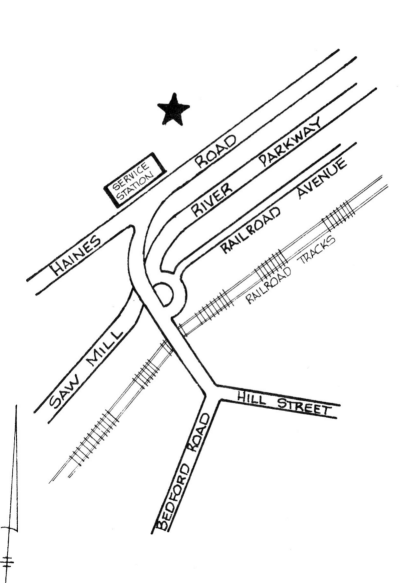

HILLCREST DRIVE CAVE

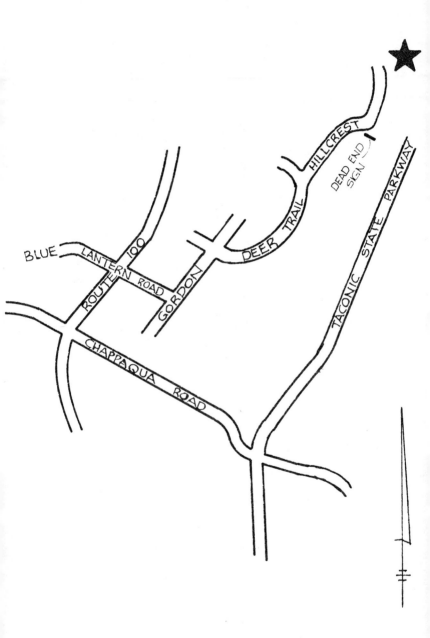

the cave is well worth the effort. One of the smallest of the Leatherman's caves, it was also used by Indians, whose arrowheads have been found within its confines. (Approximate walking time: less than 5 minutes from gas station.)

Hillcrest Drive Cave, north of Briarcliff Manor, New York. Centuries before the Leatherman trekked through the countryside, glacial action caused huge boulders and slabs of rock to come crashing down the face of a cliff. Several small caves were formed in the immediate area. Take the Chappaqua Road exit on the Taconic State Parkway and travel west until you reach Route 100. Turn right (north) on Route 100 to Blue Lantern Road. Here you make another right turn. Follow this road until you reach Gordon Avenue and make a left turn. Proceed along Gordon Avenue until you reach Deer Trail. Turn right and follow this street to Hillcrest Drive where you will find a "Dead End" sign. Continue on the black-top road past the sign for about 100 yards. The caves will be seen to your right. The one the Leatherman used is behind the huge, slab-like boulder which parallels the road. (Approximate walking time: 5 minutes from "Dead End" sign.)

4 Counterfeiter's "Factory"

The young boy sat silently in the shadowed corner of the kitchen, hoping his father would not remember his presence. Fred didn't want to go to bed yet—not now, when they were talking about the counterfeiter.

Fred had never heard the word before, but by listening carefully, he figured out that a counterfeiter was someone who made his own coins and passed them off as legal money. And such a man was operating out of a cave right here in Philipstown!

"I still don't believe it," Fred's father was saying. "Why, nobody's tried anything like that since they hanged old Jubar over in Poughkeepsie. And that was way back in 1665—more than a century ago!

"Maybe somebody found old Jubar's mine," a black-bearded man spoke up.

The five other men nodded, but not Fred's father. "If old Jubar did have a silver mine somewhere nearby, don't you think his friend, Taylor, would have found it?" he asked.

For a moment no one spoke, and only the crackling of the logs burning in the fireplace broke the silence. Then Fred's father said, "I remember my grandpa talking about Jubar and his silver mine. Seems that when the British caught Jubar, his partner Taylor ran away. Then after the Revolutionary War, Taylor returned to Philipstown. But he had no money and died a pauper. Now, if Jubar had discovered silver, Taylor would have known where, and he wouldn't have stayed penniless."

Taking the old-fashioned clay pipe from his mouth, a gray-haired man nodded as he said, "Maybe you're right about Jubar and Taylor, but how about Eleazer Gray? He found silver in the Sunk Lot back in 1772."

"Did you ever see any of it?" Fred's father shot back.

"Well, no, but Ebenezer Hopper believed the story enough to go hunting for it in 1782."

"And did Hopper find it?"

The gray-haired man shook his head.

"Just because they didn't find it doesn't mean there isn't any," Fred spoke up from the shadows. In his excitement, he had forgotten to keep still.

His father swung around in his chair, a frown on his face. "I thought I told you to go to bed," he said softly, but Fred knew it was an order.

"Yes, Pa, I'm going," he replied. "I just got so interested in what you were saying about the counterfooter..."

"Counterfeiter," his father automatically corrected.

"Oh...counterfeiter," the boy acknowledged, then hurriedly explained, "I thought if I listened, I could learn enough to help you go looking for the counterfeiter's cave."

His father's frown grew deeper with each word, and Fred scurried to the stairs, murmuring a hasty "Good night."

"You see what happens with such talk?" his father's irritated voice followed Fred upstairs. "Even my son is all set to drop everything and go traipsing over the countryside to catch a counterfeiter and find his hoard of silver in some cave that probably doesn't even exist!"

"Then you don't think there's truth to the story?" the black-haired man asked.

"I think we'd sooner find a leprechaun's pot of gold before we uncover a counterfeiter's pot of silver," Fred's father persisted.

"But all over Philipstown government agents have been asking questions about caves the counterfeiter might be using," another man spoke up. "Surely that will convince you."

Fred's father stood his ground, however. "The only thing I'm convinced of," he said, "is that if I'm not home to milk my herd of dairy cows, there'll be no silver in *my* pot!"

Exasperated, the other men left the farmhouse, after telling Fred's father where to join them the following day in case he changed his mind.

He did not change his mind, though, and young Fred was disappointed the next morning when his father told him so. Then he sent Fred out to the pasture to bring the cows in for milking. By the time the boy returned, however, all thoughts of counterfeiting and silver had fled from his mind.

"Domino is missing!" Fred called as he approached the barn.

"Domino again!" his father groaned. "Probably knocked down the weak part in the fence that I've been meaning to mend."

Fred couldn't suppress a grin over his favorite cow's antics. "Oh, she'll be back soon enough," he predicted. "She always does come home."

"She always has," the older man conceded. "But rainfall's been heavy lately and there's bogs in the low-lying areas. Best we go look for her as soon as the milking is done."

With a sigh, Fred set about milking the first cow, wishing that Domino would return before they finished. But there was no sign of the black and white cow an hour later, so they set out to check the marshy area near the lake. The wandering Domino was not there, nor was she at any of the other places they examined before returning home for dinner.

"We'd better go have a look at that swampy ground at the southeast base of the mountain," Fred's father decided as he got up from the table.

"Do you really think she might go that far?" the tired boy asked.

"Now, Fred, do I hear a reluctant tone in your voice?" his father chided. "Why, just last night you were all set to traipse all over these parts to hunt for some counterfeiter's silver. Surely Domino is just as important."

"Of course she is, Pa," Fred replied, a little ashamed of himself. "Just let me finish this piece of pie and I'll be right with you."

It was not hard going until after they had crossed over Indian Brook and began to head southeast on an old woods road. Actually the road was little more than a wide path, which had been used by timber-cutters since the area was first settled. The difficult part came when Fred's father turned off the road and headed into the dense forest of beech and oak trees.

Keeping the upgrade of the mountain to their left, they soon came to the swampy area Fred's father had mentioned earlier. The forest was silent except for the occasional call of a bird. Yet, they could not detect the telltale tinkle of the bell that Domino wore around her neck.

"She's not here, Pa," Fred spoke up, after they had stood listening for several minutes.

The man nodded. "It would seem so," he agreed. "But I wouldn't put it past that wily creature to be playing possum. Come on, we'll skirt the ridge just to make sure."

They had walked for only a few minutes when the older man stopped, narrowing his eyes to peer through the thick foliage. Fred followed his father's gaze, which was now centered on a huge mass of jumbled rocks. Fully 300 feet high, they looked as if some giant hand had pushed them down the side of the mountain.

"I had forgotten about this place," Fred's father murmured. "Haven't been here since I was younger than you, son. Come on, let's see what's up there."

The boy looked at his father, then at the rocks, then back to his father once more. "Pa, you don't think Domino went up *there*, do you?"

"No, I don't think she did," the man answered

slowly, his eyes still on the massive boulders. "Come on, let's start climbing."

"But if you don't think Domino's up there," Fred began, "then why...." He didn't finish his question because suddenly he knew why.

"The counterfeiter's cave!" he gasped.

His father shrugged his wide shoulders. "Since we're already here, no harm in checking." Then, with a somewhat sheepish grin, he added, "Guess such stories are as intriguing to grown men as they are to young boys. Anyway, I'd like to see that fellow caught before anybody else gets stuck with one of his bogus coins."

For half an hour they scrambled over, around and through the tumbled boulders until their hands were scratched and their breath burned in their throats. But there was no sign of anyone having been there before them. None of the small rock overhangs was big enough to house a man, let alone a counterfeiting operation.

Seeing the disappointment on the boy's face, Fred's father pointed out, "If such hideouts were easy to find, criminals and outlaws wouldn't be in business for very long, would they?"

The boy only nodded his head.

"Let's rest a few minutes on that flat-topped boulder over there, Fred. Then we'd best get back to hunting for Domino."

When they reached the boulder, the two of them stretched out on their backs, gazing up at the blue sky through the lace-like pattern of the leaves on the straggly trees which fought to maintain a precarious foothold in earth-filled crevices among the boulders.

His back smarted from the unevenness of the rock. Therefore, Fred shifted from his back to his belly and idly tossed pebbles into a crevice between the boulders. When he had used up all the pebbles within reach, he scooted over to the edge of the crevice to pick up those that had fallen short of the mark. Curiosity prompted him to peer down into the crevice, and then...

"Pa! Pa!" came his excited voice. "It's more than

just a crevice. I think there's a. . .a *cave* down there!"

Fred was already beginning to lower himself into the dim passageway below when his father's voice halted him.

"Hold up there, Fred," he said urgently. "If it is a cave, we don't know what's in it. And it's too dark in there to be exploring without some kind of light."

Reluctantly the boy sat back, the down-turned corners of his mouth displaying his renewed disappointment.

"Now, I didn't say we weren't going in," his father told him. "I just said to hold it a minute."

The down-turned corners of his mouth were swept up into a wide grin as Fred helped his father toss some rocks into the cave entrance to see if any bobcats might be using it as their den. Then he gathered wild grapevines to twist into makeshift torches.

A few minutes later, they had descended the step-like rocks into the cave. Pausing only to light their torches, they proceeded into the chamber where a cool rush of air soon dried the perspiration which beaded their flushed faces.

The granite room in which they found themselves was about 20 feet long and 4 feet wide. It ended in a squared piece of rock about 5 feet high, though the ceiling itself was much higher. Peering over this rock, they discovered an upper hall, narrower than the chamber below and shorter. Clambering up, they inched their way along the narrow hallway to the end, where they felt a strong current of air.

Soon they were thrusting their torches through a cleft about chest-high in the rock wall at the back of the hallway. On the other side of the cleft was a small chamber with fairly smooth, curved walls. It was most likely caused by the action of some stream that had once rushed through from a small opening at the far end of the rock ceiling.

"Oh, Pa!" came Fred's breathless whisper. "What a grand cave!"

But they had not seen the best part. They soon

found this out when they reversed their steps and returned to the main chamber they had first entered.

To their right, the flames of their torches revealed that the floor of the cavern gradually sloped down to another nearly level chamber much larger than the others.

Without speaking, father and son scrambled over the rocky slope to the lower chamber, where they stood in stunned amazement. Fred's eyes darted from the crude fireplace to the accumulation of man-made tools surrounding it.

"Why, it's . . . it's the . . ."

"Counterfeiter's workroom," his father supplied the missing words, his own voice hoarse with surprise. Bending over, he touched a heavy iron pot. "That's a crucible for smelting ore," he explained briefly. Then he picked up a narrow piece of iron that looked something like a bullet mold. "For making the counterfeit coins, I suppose."

The sound of a falling rock startled them, and they spun around to face the slope they had just descended. The small rock which had made the sound came to rest not far from their feet.

There was fear in the man's eyes as well as Fred's as they stood there in suspenseful silence.

When no further sound came, they both expelled their breath in a noisy, relieved sigh. They had probably dislodged the rock on their way down the incline.

Then Fred's father spoke. "We'd best be getting out of here before the counterfeiter returns. Touch nothing, son — the government agents will need all this as evidence."

Fred needed no urging, and they were soon out of the cave, descending the tumbled rocks and heading back to their farm.

Just as they were hitching the team to the wagon which would take them to Peekskill, where they would report their discovery, they heard a low but demanding "moo" coming from the barn.

Looking up, they met the brown-eyed gaze of

Domino, who was standing by the barn door, waiting to be milked.

"You're a little late for morning milking and a little early for evening milking," Fred's father observed with a chuckle. "But I guess those government agents can wait long enough for me to milk you before we go."

"After all," Fred laughed, "if it wasn't for Domino, we'd have nothing to report, would we, Pa?"

Not long after his "factory" was discovered, a man named Henry Holmes was arrested, tried for counterfeiting, and sentenced to seven years in prison. Strangely enough, he might never have been caught had he restricted the circulation of his coins to the rural districts around Philipstown. Since farmers of those days rarely had the opportunity to handle much "hard money," few of them could tell the difference between a government-minted coin and a counterfeit one.

However, in time Holmes extended his field of operation to such towns as Peekskill, Newburgh, Fishkill and Poughkeepsie, where the counterfeit coins were soon detected and government agents notified.

When the story of Holmes' illegal "Factory" became known, people began searching the cave. They hoped to discover the silver with which Holmes coated the base metal of his counterfeit coins.

In time, the cave became known as the Money Hole, though no silver—or even any of the counterfeit coins—was ever found. (At least no such discovery was ever made public.) People also searched for the mine from which Holmes extracted his silver-bearing ore but, again, none was ever found. Perhaps it was discovered by someone who did not report his find. Perhaps it is still there waiting to be discovered. No one knows.

Over the years, Money Hole Cave continued to play host to many searchers, but, aside from the broken lip of a crucible and other fragments from Holmes' activities there, such explorations were fruitless and the cave was almost forgotten.

Situated on land that is now part of the Taconic State Park system, the cave is in a remote area and almost impossible to find if you don't know exactly where to look. Fortunately, one long-time resident, Fred F. Reeve, remembered visiting it many years ago, and in 1973 he led a party to the Money Hole. Though there is no distinct footpath to the cave, tree markers have how been installed to guide anyone interested in visiting this intriguing and history-rich cave.

How to Get There

Money Hole Cave, off Indian Brook Road, near Garrison, New York. (Because of the lack of a distinct path to the cave, directions to it are given in great detail.) Going north on Route 9 about 8 miles from Peekskill, take the right-hand turn at the sign pointing the way to the Bird and Bottle Restaurant. Continue down the road and make a left turn past the restaurant. Cross the small bridge over Indian Brook, then make a right turn into Indian Brook Road. Proceed up this road for a little more than half a mile until you come to a wide path on the right-hand side of the road. There is a beech tree with a yellow state park sign on the east side of the path (to your left as you enter the path), and a rock cairn on the west side, about 10 feet from the path. Continue up this path for about a quarter of a mile until you see a tree growing out of the split in a low rock on your left. Near this, on a larger tree, you will see the first marker—an aluminum disc nailed about 6 feet up on the trunk of the tree.

Turn left off the path and proceed to the next marker near a break in an old stone fence. Go through this break, bearing right to the next marker, then swing left as you see other markers up ahead. You will pass a small

Money Hole Cave

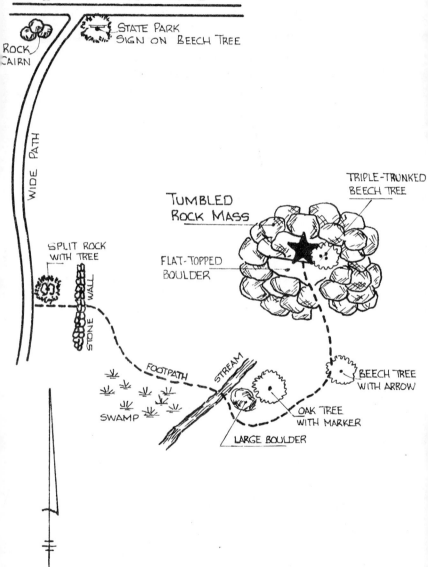

Indian Brook Road

Rock Cairn

State Park Sign on Beech Tree

Wide Path

Split Rock with Tree

Stone Wall

Tumbled Rock Mass

Triple-Trunked Beech Tree

Flat-Topped Boulder

Footpath

Stream

Swamp

Beech Tree with Arrow

Oak Tree with Marker

Large Boulder

swamp to your right. Follow the aluminum markers, cross a narrow stream (usually dry during the summer), then go straight up the hill on the opposite bank. Part way up you will see a large boulder behind which is an oak tree bearing a marker.

Continue up the hill, veering left after the oak tree marker (going almost due east of the oak tree). The next marker is on a beech tree at the base of a tumbled rock mass about 300 feet high. Go almost straight up the tumbled rocks to a beech tree marked with an aluminum arrow pointing to the left.

Veer left up the rocks. About halfway up you will see a huge boulder jutting out from the surrounding mass. Upon reaching the top of this flat-surfaced boulder, you will see a triple-trunked beech tree growing out from among the rocks in back of the boulder (the end facing the rock mass). On this tree is another aluminum arrow, which points down to the cave entrance (between the flat-topped boulder and the surrounding rocks) about 10 feet in front of the tree.

Unless you are right on top of the cave, you cannot see it, as the entrance shaft descends into the rocks about 12 feet. (There are small ledges which provide adequate "steps" and handholds, but it is a difficult descent for anyone younger than 8 or 9 years old.) The cave then extends horizontally from this natural shaft. (Approximate walking time: 30 minutes from the start of path at Indian Brook Road.)

5 Home for a Hermitess

The January wind was like an angry drover. It screeched and shrieked and pushed the snow, which was stampeding over the hills and valleys of Westchester County. It was particularly bad in North Salem, where some of the hills rose high enough to be called mountains, and by late afternoon not a person could be seen on the streets of the village. Only the yellow rectangles of light from the windows of the houses gave evidence that the community was not deserted.

Suddenly another larger rectangle was added to those lights already studding the snowy premature darkness. The door to the Darius Benedict home opened and revealed two figures.

"You must not attempt it, Miss Sarah," came a worried voice. "The snow is already too deep."

"Thank you, my friend, but I must return to my home."

"At least stay the night," the man urged, "and go back in the morning when there's light enough to see by."

The woman only shook her head.

"You'll never find the trail," the man protested in a last effort to keep the old woman from setting out in the storm.

47

A fleeting smile touched the corners of the woman's mouth. "After thirty years, I need no trail to guide my steps," she said quietly. "Now I must go."

Helplessly, the man watched until the bent form crossed over the patch of snow illuminated by the light from the open door, and then disappeared into the darkness beyond.

When he returned inside, his wife looked at him with stricken eyes. "You could not persuade her to stay?"

"No," the man replied. Then, as if to convince himself, he added, "But she's made it safely through other snowstorms. Remember the one in 1800?"

"That was nine years ago when Sarah was younger and stronger," his wife pointed out. "It's different now."

It was different, indeed, the old woman thought, as she headed into the face of the storm. She, too, had been remembering the many winters she had spent in the cave on the mountain, where blizzards often kept her snowbound for weeks at a time.

Somehow this storm seemed more violent, as if determined to cut off her very breathing by the snowflakes being hurled into her face in suffocating profusion. As for the bitter wind which drove them, it was like none she could recall.

Still she trudged on, her legs already aching from the effort of breaking a path through the knee-deep snow. It would be better once she began to ascend the mountain. The wind might be stronger there, but it probably had swept most of the snow from the steep slope and deposited it in the valley through which she now struggled.

The bitter cold had already penetrated her ragged clothing, and she could no longer feel any sensation in her hands and feet. But this wasn't so bad; frostbite was no stranger to her. It was the wind which bothered her the most—the terrible, never-ceasing wind which seemed to cut off her very breathing.

As she skirted the pond at the base of the mountain, she paused to look back, though she knew there was nothing to see except the snow eddying through the gaunt, winter-blackened trees.

Perhaps Darius Benedict had been right. Perhaps she should have stayed for the night. But she would not be comfortable there — only in her cave could she be at ease. Only there did she feel secure. Of course, the Benedicts could not understand that there was no danger in the darkness. Away from the man-made light of the farmhouse, it was not really that dark, and even in the swirling snow, she was able to discern enough not to lose her way.

No, it was not the darkness that posed the threat. It was the wind — the bitter, breath-stopping wind.

Though she had come more than half the way, she still had the hardest part of her journey before her — the stiff climb up the side of the mountain. How could she accomplish this when she could barely catch her breath — when her lungs ached as if an iron spike had been thrust between her ribs?

She must rest for a while. There was no other way. Yet to stop in the middle of a blizzard was to risk death. If she were to fall asleep. . . .

A dread fear suddenly stabbed through her. It was a fear worse than any she had ever known — even worse than that night thirty years ago when the British officer. . . .

No, she would not think of that. It did not matter now, after all these years. What mattered now was getting home — and home was up the side of the wind-lashed mountain.

Not far ahead there was a small hollow at the base of the mountain. It would offer protection from the wind, and she could at least catch her breath before starting up the mountain.

By the time she had reached the hollow, her whole body was trembling from the effort. She would feel stronger, though, after a few minutes of rest. Strangely enough, she was no longer cold — only tired, very very tired. . .

The blizzard blew on all night and almost buried

the village of North Salem beneath a blue-shadowed layer of snow. Therefore, it was several days before any of the villagers ventured out as far as the tiny cave on Long Pond Mountain. When they did, however, they noticed there were no tracks in the snow around the home of the hermitess, Sarah Bishop. Thinking she might be lying ill inside and in need of assistance, they entered the cave, only to find it was empty.

Alarmed now, they set out to search for her, following her well-known route down the southern slope of the mountain. When they reached the base, they found her frozen body in the hollow where she had sought refuge from the relentless wind. Sarah Bishop was dead — but not the legend of her mysterious and solitary ways.

It was toward the end of the Revolutionary War that Sarah Bishop first appeared in what was then called Lower Salem. In those days, it was unusual enough for a young woman to be traveling alone, but even more so for someone who had obviously been raised in a well-to-do and cultured family. For not only were Sarah's clothes fashionable and made of costly materials, but her manners were refined and gave evidence of good breeding.

Attempts by the townspeople to find out where she came from and why she had left were politely but firmly rebuffed. Nor would Sarah speak of her past to the deacons of the Presbyterian Church for whom she soon started to work as a seamstress.

Since no family had enough to keep her occupied at all times, Sarah would go from house to house — a day here, a week there — spinning and knitting as well as sewing. Whatever the chore, her work was always satisfactory, except for one odd thing: she preferred to work at night and sleep during the day.

The superstitious folk of those days might have condemned her for this, except for the fact that Sarah was a devout Christian. She always attended church on Sundays and was often seen reading her Bible during the week. Therefore, her odd behavior was tolerated, and her nimble fingers were much in demand at a time when all clothing was made by hand.

Before long, however, Sarah began disappearing from the village. At first her absences were for a few days, then weeks would pass before she returned to seek the odd jobs the villagers usually had available.

In time it was discovered that she was living in a tiny, wedge-shaped cave, which measured about four feet high and six feet deep. Extending from one side of the mouth of the cave, she had constructed a stone wall. On top of this she had placed branches, interspersed with twigs and bark, that sloped toward the rock roof of the cave, thereby enlarging her home somewhat. A small entrance was left in this stone and branch wall, which she closed off at night with pieces of bark she had stripped from decayed trees.

There was not even the most primitive of furnishings within. She slept on the floor of the cave and used a low projection from the rock wall as a pillow. As for utensils, the only things she had were an old pewter basin and a dipper which had been made from a gourd. Oddest of all was the fact that she was never known to build a fire, even during the harsh winters. When the cave was examined after her death, there was no evidence that a fire had ever been built.

As the years passed by, she used the fertile ground in front of her cave to plant a few peach trees, along with a garden containing potatoes, cucumbers and beans. These, plus the wild grapes, berries and nuts which grew in abundance all over the mountain, formed the main part of her diet, for Sarah once told someone she ate very little meat. In the winter, she subsisted on those foods she had stored in a cleft in the rock wall of her cave.

Perhaps because they sensed that she meant them no harm, the woodland animals were not frightened of her, and she made pets of many of them. One rather fanciful report held that she even kept a pet rattlesnake which she fed milk she brought from the village.

Her visits to North Salem grew less frequent as

time went on, and sometimes she was not seen there from late fall until early spring, having stayed all winter in her solitary cave. However, when spring came and it was easier to travel, she would come to North Salem on Sunday to attend church. She kept a few dresses (the only ones left from the wardrobe she had brought with her) at the home of a friend. There she would change from her everyday attire of pieced-together rags to an out-moded black dress. Then she would go to church and slip into one of the back pews. After the service, she would return to the friend's house, change back to her ragged clothes, and return to her cave on the mountain.

Though timid by nature, she would converse pleasantly enough with those she came in contact with, but she never referred to her life before her arrival in North Salem. People were curious, however, and began putting together various bits of information.

She was often seen sitting on a high rock near her cave, gazing south across the Sound to where the hills of Long Island rose in the distance. Why did she do this? Some said it was only because of the spectacular view, but others maintained that she had chosen her mountain hermitage specifically because she could look back on what had once been her home.

Sarah Bishop, it was said, had been born into a prominent Long Island family, whose wealth insured her a life of ease until the Revolutionary War broke out. Then in 1776, George Washington was forced to retreat from Long Island and the British took over, laying waste to the homes of many who sympathized with the American cause. The Bishop home was one of those burned, and young Sarah had become the victim of an abusive English officer.

Fleeing to the hills of northern Westchester County, she spent the rest of her life there, growing to love solitude more and more, yet never forgetting the home where she had known so much joy as a child and such tragedy as a young woman.

Such is the legend Sarah Bishop left behind her on

Sarah Bishop Cave

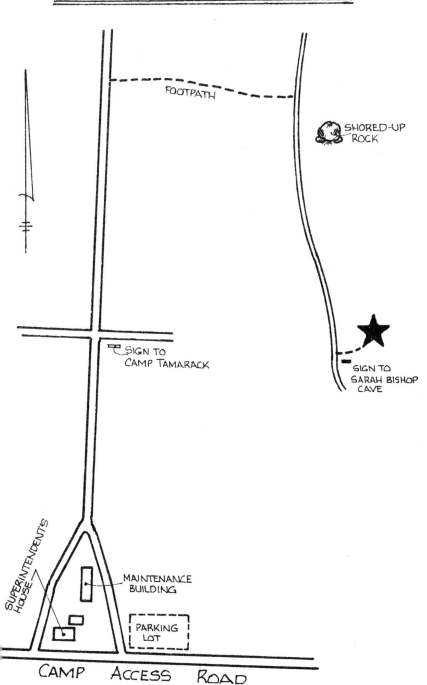

that snowy night back in 1809 — a legend which takes on a special meaning when one visits her tiny cave on Long Pond Mountain, and then views the hills of Long Island rising like a misty memory on the far horizon.

How to Get There

Sarah Bishop Cave, near Mountain Lakes Camp, North Salem, New York. (The easiest route to Sarah Bishop Cave is through land maintained by Westchester County. During July and August the county runs Mountain Lakes Camp on this land, and, therefore, it is best to visit the cave during those months when camp is not in session: September through June.) Going north on Route 121/124, make a right turn at Grants Corners onto Hawley Road. Then make a left turn at the next crossroad. There you will see a sign pointing the way to Mountain Lakes Camp. Keep on this road until you come to the camp entrance. (Permission to enter the camp should be obtained from the superintendent, whose house stands between the two entrance roads.) Proceed north up the paved road into the camp for about a quarter of a mile. You will pass a sign pointing to Camp Tamarack — do not turn here. Continue north on the road until you reach a footpath that veers off to the right (east).

Follow this footpath until it crosses another wider path running north and south. Go south (to your right) along the second path, passing a huge boulder on your left that has been shored up by rocks and cement. Continue along the path until you see a small wooden sign on your left saying "Sarah Bishop Cave." Turn left as the sign directs. About thirty feet up this narrow path is the cave. (Approximate walking time: 40 minutes from camp entrance.)

Sassacus Finds a Refuge

6

The late afternoon sunshine sent long shadowy fingers through the forest. Each one seemed to be reaching out to hold back the lone figure that was sliding and stumbling down the steep slope to the rushing stream below.

In the muted thunder of the waterfall, the man's labored breathing could not be heard as he paused to rest on the bank of the stream, his black eyes studying the slope he had just come down.

There was no way he could mask the broken branches he had crashed into or the imprint of his moccasins in the soft earth. Even if it weren't for his wounded leg, he was too exhausted right now to go back and spread leaves over the telltale signs of his descent.

At least there were no bloodstains to provide scarlet clues for any pursuers. For that he could thank the yarrow plant which had been plentiful all along the many miles he and his band had traveled. Each time he had stopped to rest, he had crushed some of the white and purple flowers between two stones and applied the powder to the worst of his wounds. And the wounds were many—caused by the final bloody battle with Captain Mason, as well as by his subsequent flight from the field where most of his Pequot warriors had met death.

As if the memory of that last battle had renewed his energy, the wounded Indian rose to his feet. Captain Mason may have annihilated most of his warriors, but not all. Some of them—almost thirty—had survived to follow their leader west into the land of the Mohawk. With luck, they would find refuge somewhere until their wounds were healed. Then he, Sassacus, Chief of the Pequots, would lead them into battle once more.

But first he must find that refuge.

The discovery came sooner than he expected. For as he crossed the small stream fed by the waterfall, Sassacus slipped on the moss-covered rocks. The churning water had tumbled him almost beneath the waterfall before he managed to reach the rocks which lined the opposite bank. Shivering, he clambered over the rocks, the icy spray from the waterfall stinging his already lacerated body.

It was then that he saw the cave behind the waterfall. Ignoring the blood that pulsed from his reopened wounds, Sassacus carefully proceeded along the narrow ledge which bordered the high stone walls of the ravine. A few moments later he was past the curtain of white-flecked water and standing inside the cave.

There was no other human being around to hear the exultant cry of the Pequot chief, but even if there had been the roar of the cascading water outside the cave would have overwhelmed the sound. Knowing this, Sassacus shouted again—this time the high, keening war cry of the Pequots. He had found a place of refuge! He had not been defeated after all—this, he vowed, the white settlers would soon find out.

Returning over the trail he had been scouting, Sassacus soon had his small band of warriors secreted in the cave behind the waterfall. For many weeks they remained there, venturing out only to gather herbs to heal their wounds, while an abundance of berries augmented their diet of fish and other wildlife.

Always they spoke of returning to wage war against the white man who had taken over their land. The hatred of Sassacus was especially bitter, for the Dutch had killed his father, the former Chief Wopigwooit, at the main village of the Pequots near what was later to be called Hartford, Connecticut.

Upon the death of his father, Sassacus had become chief of the Pequots. A short time afterward, in October 1634, those who knew of his hatred for the white men were amazed to learn that Sassacus had proposed a treaty of friendship to the governor of Massachusetts Bay Colony. In it, he offered to give up all claim to the vast Pequot lands — from Narragansett Bay to the Hudson River and east to include most of Long Island. In exchange, a certain smaller area was to be guaranteed to the Pequots on which no white man would set foot.

The sachems who had pledged their loyalty to Sassacus soon determined that their wily chief almost certainly had a sinister motive behind this offer of friendship. Only Uncas, Chief of the Mohicans, did not realize this, and he vowed to exterminate Sassacus for siding with the enemy.

Whatever Sassacus' reasons might have been for proposing the treaty, he had no intention of abandoning his belligerent ways, and within two years a full-scale war had broken out between the Pequots and the white colonists.

The conflict was short but bloody, ending less than a year later at what is now New London, Connecticut, when the Pequots were virtually wiped out. Leading his few remaining warriors, Sassacus had managed to slip through the land of his enemies, the Mohicans, and make his way to Mohawk country where he found the cave behind the waterfall.

When his warriors were strong once more, Sassacus ventured out, confident of his safety among the Mohawks. But the Pequot chief was not trusted even by those he considered his allies, for he had been known to attack neighboring tribes.

This may have been the reason the Mohawks turned against him. More than likely, it was because of the large amount of wampum (beaded ornaments used as money by the Indians) which Sassacus carried with him — a treasure that might well turn a former friend into an enemy. In any event, before the year 1637 had drawn to a close, the scalp of Sassacus — along with those of his brother and five lesser Pequot chiefs — had been sent by the Mohawks to the governor of Massachusetts Bay Colony.

The last great chief of the Pequots had been defeated, not by the white men who he hated, but by those of his own people who he trusted.

Over the centuries, the cave where Sassacus had sought refuge was visited by many people who saw in its vaulted entrance a replica of the Gothic arch which graced many churches and cathedrals. So it was that this historic cave with its magnificent waterfall became known as the Dover Stone Church.

The Gothic arch is still there, but the waterfall that once curtained its entrance, and formed a spectacular cascade of icicles in the winter, has fallen victim to the action of its own water. In time, the swiftly running water cut a channel through the ledge of rock that formed the roof of the cave, until the waterfall spilled into the cavern from the rear instead of over the top.

The curtain of water that hid Sassacus and his warriors may be gone today, but the Dover Stone Church is still a spectacular sight. The cave itself is about 60 feet long, 27 feet wide and 30 feet high. Its inner walls are scored and scoured with unusual designs from the action of the water. In the rear, the icy water spills down into the cave and forms a shallow stream. This stream flows through the cave and exits in another miniature waterfall divided by a huge boulder — a fitting monument to Sassacus, the last of the Pequot chiefs.

Dover Stone Church Cave

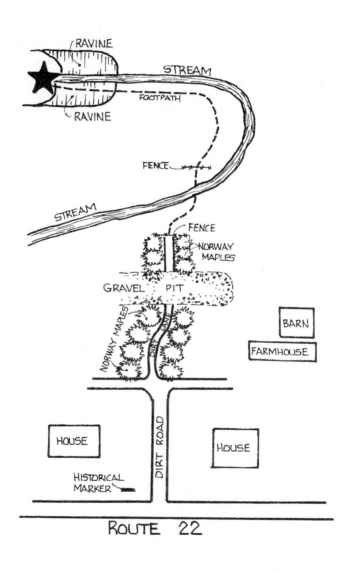

RAVINE

STREAM

FOOTPATH

RAVINE

FENCE

STREAM

FENCE

NORWAY MAPLES

GRAVEL PIT

NORWAY MAPLES

DIRT LANE

BARN

FARMHOUSE

DIRT ROAD

HOUSE

HOUSE

HISTORICAL MARKER

ROUTE 22

How to Get There

Dover Stone Church, off Route 22, Dover Plains, New York. (Although this cave is on private property, the owner usually does not mind well-behaved visitors who wish to see this unique and historic site. Request permission from Mr. Palmer of Dover Plains.) Almost in the center of the small town of Dover Plains, there is a historical marker commemorating the cave and its famous inhabitant Sassacus. The marker is on the west side (on your left going north) of Route 22. A few feet north of the marker a dirt road leads west up a short hill. Follow this dirt road until it becomes a lane lined by lovely old Norway maples. Farther on, the lane is cut off by a gravel pit which can be traversed by descending its slope at the north end. You then climb out of the pit where the lane—still lined by Norway maples—resumes on the other side.

A broken-down fence must be scrambled over or through, then the lane ends in a footpath through a meadow. The footpath is interrupted by a stream, but there are stepping stones to facilitate crossing. Resume the footpath on the other side of the stream and cross still another old fence. The path then enters the ravine, which terminates at the Dover Stone Church. (Approximate walking time: 20 minutes from the highway.)

7 The Dens of Claudius Smith

"Claudius, you will die like a trooper's horse — with your shoes on!"

The ominous prediction hung in the air like a bone-chilling fog as the angry woman pointed an accusing finger at her dark-haired stepson.

"You say you're a Tory," the woman continued, "and that your sympathies are with the British. Well, let me tell you, robbing cattle and horses and harming people proves where your sympathies really lie — with Claudius Smith and no place else!"

Without denying her accusation, the man rose from his chair by the kitchen fire, his dark eyes glinting with sparks more dangerous than those exploding from the fresh pine knots on the hearth. For a brief moment he towered over the small woman, and she could not help but shiver. Then with a few long strides of his powerful legs, Claudius Smith left the house to rejoin his gang of cowboys — so named because of their habit of making off with other people's cattle.

For a long time Claudius Smith did not return to his stepmother's house, but it was not difficult for her to keep track of him. Bold and daring, he did not care who knew of his marauding ways. And before the Revolutionary War was three years old, people spoke of him in

frightened whispers as "the scourge of the Ramapos."

The Ramapo Mountains extend from northern New Jersey into southern New York, and in many parts they are as wild today as when Claudius Smith preyed on the isolated farms and villages which dotted their rugged slopes and verdant valleys.

Even after two centuries, this notorious outlaw remains an enigma. Was he really a fervent Tory concerned only in aiding the British to win the war? Or was he only a malicious freebooter, who used the Revolutionary War as his excuse for pillage? Could it be, as some claim, that he was a latter-day Robin Hood who stole from the rich to give to the poor?

No one knows for certain, and so it is that the saga of Claudius Smith lives on today, with people still seeking the treasure he supposedly hid somewhere in the Ramapo Mountains.

There is very little to tell of his early years, except that he was born in Brookhaven, Long Island, and later moved to what is now Monroe, New York. Some people say he was a vicious young man, but there is no public record of any misbehavior until July 1777 — one year after the Revolutionary War began — when he was arrested in Kingston for "stealing oxen belonging to the Continent." Transferred to the jail at Goshen, New York, he promptly escaped, and from then on his short but violent career is a matter of history.

Gathering about him a band of equally lawless men, including three of his own sons, Claudius Smith established his headquarters in a set of caves deep within what is today Harriman State Park.

If he had built them himself, the caves could not have been more perfect for the nature of his "business." The upper cave is formed by a horizontal crack at the base of an imposing cliff. It is 30 feet long, 8 feet deep and 8 feet high at its tallest point. Part way across the entrance, Smith built a protective wall of rock, the remains of which can still be seen.

From this cave a winding passageway, with an excellent observation post about a third of the way up, leads through the rocks to the top of the cliff. From the crest of the cliff the countryside can be seen for miles around — a distinct advantage for anyone who fears pursuit.

The second cave, a short distance to the east and down the hill, is not as tall, but is wider and deeper. This was used to stable the outlaws' horses and perhaps, occasionally, some of the cattle they stole. In later years, this cave, called the Horsestable, was discovered to contain many prehistoric Indian artifacts. Apparently, Indians had once made this cave their home, too.

There are other Ramapo Mountain caves which Claudius Smith used, including a rock shelter farther to the southeast, but the two just mentioned are the largest. It was here that the Smith gang plotted their many forays against the settlers, sometimes going as far as New Jersey.

Each raid was carefully planned by Smith, and more than one historian has mentioned that "he conducted his expeditions with such cautiousness as scarcely to be suspected until in the very execution of them; and if a sudden descent was made upon him, by some bold stroke or wily maneuver he would successfully evade his pursuers and make his escape." In fact, when he was finally apprehended, it was not during a raid, but when he was asleep in a house on Long Island, many miles away from the scene of his crimes.

These crimes consisted mainly of stealing cattle and horses, which were later sold to the British then occupying New York City. Nor was Claudius Smith averse to robbing valuable articles from the houses he "visited," though few of the farmers he raided had much in the way of worldly possessions other than their livestock.

One house which did contain valuable silver and pewter was that of a Captain Woodhull, who was away on duty with the Continental Army when Claudius Smith "called" late one night in October 1778.

The quick-witted Mrs. Woodhull realized the gang must be after the fine set of silver the family possessed.

And in the time it took for Smith and his men to break down the barred door, she hid the silver and other valuables beneath her small daughter who was lying in a cradle.

The outlaws searched the house from top to bottom, but did not approach the lady of the house, who was trying to calm her fretful daughter (fretful, no doubt, from being forced to lie on the lumpy silver).

This is the only known time that Claudius Smith was thwarted, and though he might have suspected Mrs. Woodhull had hidden the silver he sought, he was not one to assault a defenseless woman.

Stories like this led to the legend that, while he might be the biggest cattle thief in the Ramapos, Claudius Smith also was a gentleman of generosity and hospitality.

The latter trait was surprisingly displayed to a member of the "opposition," a man named Judge Bodle. This happened on the day after the British captured Fort Montgomery. Retreating from the scene of the American defeat, the judge was headed for his home in Orange County when he met Claudius Smith. Since the two men knew each other, the judge was understandably fearful of what the Tory outlaw might do to him.

Alone and on foot, exhausted from the disastrous battle of the day before, there was no way the judge could escape. Therefore, he walked up to Claudius Smith as if it were an everyday occurrence for them to meet on this lonely road.

To the judge's amazement, the outlaw bid him a cordial good morning, then said, "Mr. Bodle, you are weary with walking. Go to my dwelling yonder," and he pointed to a spot a short distance from the road. "Ask my wife to give you a breakfast, and tell her that I sent you."

Yes, Claudius Smith could show compassion for his avowed enemies. Moreover, he had his own brand of chivalry when it came to women. This was made even more evident a short time later when he heard of the sad plight of Mrs. James McClaughry.

Mrs. McClaughry's husband, a colonel in Washington's army, had been captured by the British when they overran Fort Montgomery. Taken to New York City, the hapless colonel was allowed to write to his wife. In his letter he asked her to send him some money in order to buy a few of the comforts he was being denied as a prisoner.

The poor woman had no ready cash and asked the wealthy Abimal Youngs to lend her some. Figuring that he would never get his money back, Youngs refused the request. Now frantic, Mrs. McClaughry gathered together what valuables she possessed, including her shoe buckles, and pawned them. This became public knowledge, and when Claudius Smith learned who had been responsible for the woman's humiliation, he and his gang paid a "call" on Abimal Youngs one dark night.

Upon their demand that he surrender his money, Youngs refused, certain they would never find it because he had it carefully hidden. Undaunted, Claudius Smith ordered that the uncooperative Youngs be strung up to the well pole. Before Youngs stopped breathing, they let him down and warned that if he did not reveal the hiding place of his money, they would hang him for good.

Youngs still refused.

Two more times they hanged him, but he remained silent. Perhaps the wily miser knew that Smith, despite all his other crimes, was not a murderer—and he was right.

Giving up in disgust, Claudius Smith finally ordered that Youngs be released. Before riding off, however, he and his gang took all Youngs' valuable papers, such as bonds and mortgages.

Youngs never recovered his papers. Many months later, when Claudius Smith was standing on the gallows platform ready to be hanged, Youngs pushed his way through the crowd and begged the doomed man to tell him where the papers were. But Claudius Smith had not forgotten the way Youngs had treated Mrs. McClaughry. With the noose already around his neck, his voice rang out, "Mr. Youngs, this is no time to talk about papers. Meet me in the next world and I will tell you all about them."

Part of this bravado may have come from Smith's hope that his gang would rescue him, and as he spoke his eyes searched the winter-gray hills to the east of Goshen. He was confident that his men had not attempted to rescue him earlier only because an order had been given to his jailer for him "to shoot Smith, if an attack upon the prison was likely to succeed in his liberation."

It had only been by a freak accident that Claudius Smith had been captured at all. In the early fall of 1778, Smith's gang committeed a series of robberies. During one of these robberies, a Major Nathaniel Strong was shot to death, and Governor Clinton of New York offered a reward of $1,200 for Smith's arrest.

In those days such a sum of money was a small fortune, and Claudius Smith prudently decided he had better go into hiding. Rather than choose the solitary seclusion of one of his Ramapo caves, he headed for British-held New York City, where he thought he would be welcome. But even though his "cowboy" activities had aided the British, his reception there was far from warm, and he continued on to Long Island. There he boarded at a widow's house in Smithtown.

The coldness of the British in New York had made him wary, and so he kept his identity a secret. He probably would have succeeded, too, if it were not for Major John Brush.

Major Brush had been a wealthy landowner in Long Island, when the British had taken over. However, he had been forced to move to Connecticut due to his loyalty to the American cause.

Periodically he slipped back to Long Island to oversee his property, which he had left in the care of tenants. It was on just such a trip that he spotted Claudius Smith. Returning to Connecticut, Brush rounded up four other men, and together they rowed a whaleboat back across Long Island Sound.

It was almost midnight, and Claudius Smith was sound asleep in bed, when the men stealthily entered his room. After a brief struggle, during which Smith attempted to grab the pistols he kept beneath his pillow, he was tied securely and taken to the whaleboat, which immediately set out across the Sound.

Strangely enough, Claudius Smith was not tried for murder, even though one of his last robberies had resulted in the death of Major Strong. Instead, he was indicted "for burglary at the house of John Earle; for robbery at the house of Ebenezer Woodhull; for robbery of the dwelling and still-house of William Bell."

On January 13, 1779, he was tried and convicted at Goshen, New York. His execution was set for January 22. On that cold day, Smith, resplendent in "a suit of rich broadcloth with silver buttons," mounted the gallows.

After he had contemptuously told Abimal Youngs he would meet him in the next world, Claudius Smith must have thought of the dark prophecy his stepmother had made so many months before. For just as the noose was tightened, he deliberately kicked off his shoes, determined that he would not die "like a trooper's horse."

Then the rope grew taut and Claudius Smith was no more.

But legends do not die so easily, especially when — in an effort to deter others from following the outlaw trail — Claudius Smith's skull was supposedly placed over the doorway of the courthouse at Goshen. Legend says it remains to this day, as does the booty reportedly buried in one of the many Ramapo caves he used.

As for his gang, his son William and another member had been shot to death before Claudius Smith was executed, while his son James was executed at Goshen a short time after his father. Only Richard, his youngest son, and a few others of his outlaw band outwitted the law and escaped to Nova Scotia.

Many years later, the sons of some of these outlaws returned to the Ramapos to hunt for the stolen articles which had been buried. Though they had written instruc-

tions from their fathers on where to look, they found only some stolen muskets and before long they returned to Canada.

Since then many people have tried to find the treasure of Claudius Smith, but the wild Ramapos have kept their secret — if indeed there ever was a treasure at all.

How to Get There

Claudius Smith Cave and the Horsestable, Harriman State Park, near Tuxedo, New York. (A strenuous hike, much of it uphill, but well worth it.) Go north on Route 17 through Tuxedo, New York. Turn right (east) just past the Tuxedo Railroad Station — also a police barracks — on the east side of the road. Follow the turn-off road across the Erie Railroad tracks. Then go under the New York Thruway bridge to East Village Road. At this point, go left up the incline almost to the end of Grove Drive. On the right you will see a trail leading up into the woods which is marked with a red dot on the trees. (This is called the Ramapo-Dunderberg Trail and is well marked.)

Continue along the trail. You will pass a fine overlook of the surrounding country. A short distance from this point the trail turns to the right and goes up an old woods road. Follow this until you come to a crossing. Here the red dot trail goes to the left, while another trail marked with a red bar continues up the hill. (Be careful not to confuse the red dot with the red bar.)

Continue up the hill, taking the red bar trail (which is the Tuxedo-Mount Ivy Trail), until you see the Claudius Smith cave up ahead at the base of the cliff. Farther along the red bar trail, which turns to the right, you will find the Horsestable. (Approximate walking time: 45 minutes from start of the trail on Grove Drive to Claudius Smith cave; a few more minutes to the Horsestable.)

CLAUDIUS SMITH CAVE
AND THE HORSESTABLE

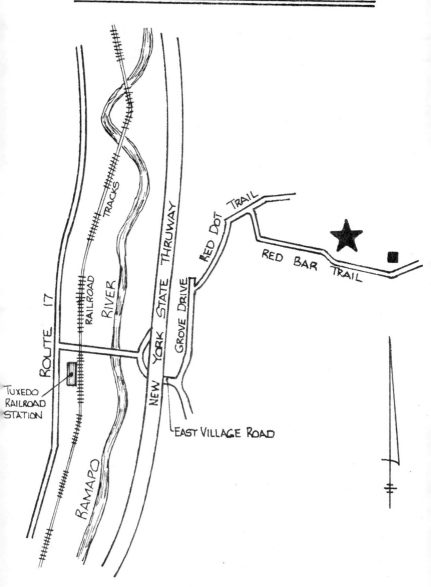

Horse Stable Rock Shelter

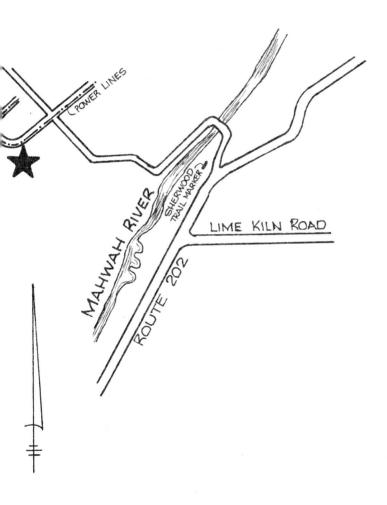

POWER LINES

MAHWAH RIVER

SHERWOOD TRAIL MARKER

LIME KILN ROAD

ROUTE 202

Horse Stable Rock Shelter, Harriman State Park, near Wesley Chapel, New York. (Not to be confused with Horse-stable Cave to the west, this rock shelter is by no means as imposing as the two main caves, but as an observation post it is unsurpassed.) Going north on Route 202 through Wesley Chapel, just past Lime Kiln Road, you will see a small sign on the left-hand (west) side of the road marked "Sherwood Trail." Follow the trail down the slope, heading north, to where the trail crosses the Mahwah River. The trail curves around to the south along the opposite (west) river bank. Then it veers to the right, ascending the hill. Farther along, the trail goes off to the left for a short distance, then turns once more to the right, taking the hiker uphill again (a stiff climb).

About three-quarters of the way up the hill, the trail crosses a power line. Turn left on the path following the power line about 200 yards along the slope of the mountain. Just before this path curves around again to head north, you will see a massive boulder standing alone a few feet to the left of the path.

On the eastern face of this boulder, looking out over the valley, is a shallow, fire-scarred rock shelter. The lookout post on top can be reached by climbing the boulder from the side facing the path. On top can be found numerous names and dates carved into the rock, including that of the man for whom Sherwood Trail was named. (Approximate walking time: 30 minutes from start of Sherwood Trail.)

8 Icebox for a Naturalist

High up on the southeast slope of the hill, the boy climbed over the narrow ledge he had seen from the valley below. Ignoring the elbow he had painfully scraped on the way up, he ran his hand over the blackened rocks which formed the entrance of the small cave.

Yes, this was it. This was the one he'd been searching for.

Pausing to catch his breath, he leaned his back against the rocks in order to gaze out over the rounded peaks of the Catskill Mountains, made domelike by time and nature. Bright green, blue-green, dark green, yellow-green, light green—all these and many more shades of what he thought must surely be God's favorite color were blended in the sun-drenched landscape before him.

For a brief moment, he wished someone could be with him to share the beauty he was now savoring, but then he remembered the purpose of his climb, and turned back to the cave.

Tossing in a few "just-in-case" rocks (just in case some animal was using the cave as its den), the boy waited a few minutes. Then he scrambled inside. Though the entrance was narrow, the cave widened and became higher a few feet inside—so much so that John was unable to see

how far it extended, even after his eyes had adjusted from the bright sunlight outside.

Searching in his pocket, he found the stub of a candle he had been saving, along with two of the phosphorous matches his mother kept in their farm kitchen. First he was careful to check that no errant draft of wind would endanger his precious matches. Then he struck one, jerking his head back to avoid the acrid fumes.

The candle stub sputtered with life and cast a weak, flickering light over that part of the cave walls closest to the boy. Slowly, he edged around the perimeter of the cave and found blackened rock only in one section, near where a narrow crevice in the roof served as a natural chimney.

He had been right, after all. The cave had been used before — the smoke-smudged wall proved it. But whether the cave had provided shelter for some Indian or just a farmer out hunting, John did not know. Somehow he felt sure an Indian had used it — at least that is what he wanted to believe.

John knew of many people around the town of Roxbury who had collections of Indian arrowheads. He even had a few himself that people had given him. But what he wanted most was to find some arrowheads himself, and maybe even a piece of pottery or some Indian tool. This cave would surely fulfill that dream.

As he examined the floor of the cave, John dug shallow holes here and there. Also, he pictured in his mind the Indian who must have lived here — perhaps a whole family, for the cave was certainly big enough.

A sudden clap of thunder made him look outside. He saw that great mounds of gray-bottomed clouds were surging against the blue-green peaks of the tallest mountains.

To a stranger, it might have looked like the granddaddy of all thunderstorms was about to deluge the countryside, but John knew better. Such a late afternoon cloud buildup was not unusual in the Catskills during the summer months. By evening the thunderheads would probably roll on and...

"By evening!" John almost shouted. Then he checked the position of the sun, just visible at the edge of one of the thunderheads touching a western peak.

Why, it was almost evening now. Had he been in the cave that long?

As if in answer to his question, his stomach rumbled emptily.

At home, supper would be waiting—waiting until he and his brothers had finished their chores. He had been due home long before now.

But how could he leave when he was so close to discovering the arrowheads he knew must be somewhere in the cave? If he went home now, he might never find the cave again. On the other hand, what if he didn't go home on time? What if he stayed here until he had fully explored the cave?

Duty warred with desire inside the boy, until he thought of how worried his mother would be if he did not get home right away. He remembered the night his brother Hiram had hurt his ankle at the sawmill and was three hours late. His mother, fearful that Hiram had fallen victim to one of the wild animals that still roamed the area, had sent all of them searching Old Clump Mountain and clear into the town of Roxbury.

Then there was Hiram, himself, to think of, as well as his other eight brothers and sisters. His chores would fall on their shoulders, as well as the needless worry over his welfare.

It just wasn't fair to them, John admitted with a sigh. Even if he never found the cave again, he must go home now.

Reluctantly snuffing out the candle, the boy left the cave. He paused long enough to take one last look, trying to memorize its location, before he headed home.

Due to the heavy work load at the farm, it was several weeks before John had a full day to go exploring again. By that time, the lush vegetation had changed the whole countryside. All, except the most prominent outcroppings of rocks, were masked with rich, green foliage which seemed to give (as he was later to write) "eyebrows to the faces of the hills."

John did not find the cave again, but he did find others as he grew to manhood on his father's farm near Roxbury, New York. And by the time he went off to teach school in Ulster County, during the year 1854, his love for what he called "the friendly rocks" had grown into a dream. He hoped that someday he would devote his time to writing about nature, so that others could see the beauties that he saw.

It was many years before John Burroughs was to realize his dream. However, while teaching school in such places as Illinois and New Jersey, he began to write poems and essays, many of them concerning his ever-increasing love and respect for nature. But his writing could not support a wife and family, and so in 1863 he took a job with the Treasury Department in Washington, D.C.

He held this post for ten years. During this period he wrote his first book which was about his dearest friend and fellow author, Walt Whitman. Other books were to follow, and by 1873 when he left his job in Washington, John Burroughs was a well-established author and authority on natural history.

It was then he purchased a farm, which he named Riverby, in what is now West Park, New York, on the west bank of the Hudson River. Two years later, he built a cabin retreat, called Slabsides, about a mile from his home. It was here that John Burroughs found the answer to another boyhood dream.

Right in back of Slabsides was a small cave about fifteen feet deep. It was not an Indian cave, to be sure, but it was even more interesting because of the geological story it told.

As he was to write in *Time and Change:*

A huge mass of rock, that had been planed and gouged by the glacier [from the time of the Ice Age], was detached and toppled over, turning topsy-turvy...and it lies in such a position, upheld by two rock fragments, that its glaciated surface, though protected by weather, is clearly visible. You step down two or three feet between two upholding rocks and are at the entrance of a little cave, and there before you, standing at an angle of thirty or forty degrees, is this rocky page written over with the history of the passing of the great ice plane.

The surface exposed is ten or twelve feet long, and four or five feet wide, and it is as straight and smooth, and the scratches and grooves are as sharp and distinct as if made yesterday.

I often take the college girls there who come to visit me, to show them, as I tell them, where the old ice gods left their signatures.

The girls take turns in stooping down and looking along the under surface of the rock, and feeling it with their hands, and marveling. They have read or heard about these things, but the reading or hearing made little impression upon their minds. When they see a concrete example, and feel it with their hands, they are impressed.

And so have been all the other people — including such famous men as President Theodore Roosevelt — who have visited the cave behind Slabsides.

However important the cave might be as a "lesson in geology," John Burroughs was every bit a practical man who believed — as did the Indians before him — that natural gifts were to be put to good use. Therefore, this unique little cave became his icebox, where he stored perishable food during his stays at Slabsides.

There was no air-conditioning in those days, and the small valley where Slabsides is situated could get very hot in the summer months. On days when the temperature soared, John Burroughs could be found sitting either in his "icebox" or else seated on the ledge at its entrance, beneath the huge rock slab that had been tumbled into place during a long-ago Ice Age.

Possibly at such times his thoughts would return to

his boyhood days when he had first explored "the friendly rocks." Never had he dreamed back then that someday he would have a cave of his own and be a world-famous naturalist.

Two other caves are associated with John Burroughs. One is located on Slide Mountain, the highest peak in the Catskills. But it is an arduous climb to reach it, and it has no particular significance other than being a grotto often used by hikers.

The second is in the Adirondacks on a branch of the Hudson called the Boreas River, near the town of Minerva. This cave was visited by Burroughs in 1863 and although its setting is one of beauty, it is difficult to find and there is no story attached to it. (However, for those experienced backpackers who would like to visit it, further information on its location can be found in an article entitled "In Burroughs Footsteps," in the December-January 1972-73 issue of *The Conservationist,* a periodical put out by the New York State Department of Environmental Conservation.)

How to Get There

Burroughs Cave, Slabsides, West Park, New York. (The caretaker of Slabsides is Mrs. Hugh Kelley, the granddaughter of John Burroughs. For permission to visit, contact Mrs. Kelley at West Park, New York, 12493. When convenient, she will meet visitors and show them the interior of Slabsides.) There is a historical marker commemorating Slabsides on Route 9W as you enter West Park. Heading north on Route 9W, make a left turn (west) at the marker. Cross the bridge that goes over some railroad tracks, and continue on to Floyd Ackert Road. Follow this road to the top of the hill (about half a mile), then turn left

John Burroughs' Cave

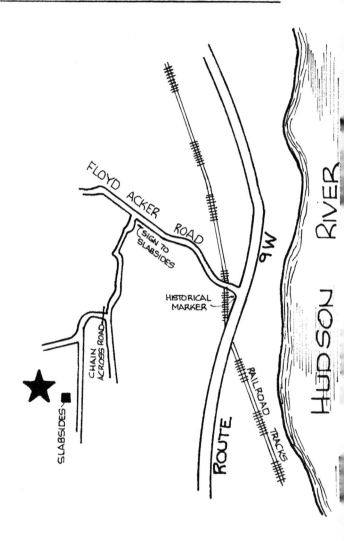

into Burroughs Drive. Continue down Burroughs Drive until you come to a chain across a wide path on your right (there are occasional signs to guide you).

Follow this wide path about one-tenth of a mile to Slabsides. The cave is behind the cabin. (Approximate walking time: 10 minutes from start of path.)

9 A Gift from The Enemy

"I'm turning into an apple!"

The distressed cry came from a young girl sitting amid a fragrant pile of apple peels and cores. Thrusting aside the knife she had been using on the fruit, nine-year-old Susan added hotly, "This new state of ours has just too many apples for me!"

Her older sister Rosemary looked up from the apple slices she was arranging in neat rows on a wooden board. "Come February," she predicted, "you'll be mighty thankful for the apples you peeled in October!"

Susan was immediately contrite. "What you say is true," she told her sister. "And dried apples are indeed delicious when there's no other fruit to be had in wintertime. It's just that it takes so long to prepare them. If only we could have one day away from these apples!"

Rosemary nodded in agreement, then gazed longingly at the autumn-tinted hills surrounding their small farm in the Hudson Highlands. She, too, would like to forget the mounds of apples, and take a walk in the brilliant October sunshine. But it was just such sunshine that was needed to dry the apple slices in order to preserve them. So with a sigh, the older girl turned back to her work.

It was a few minutes before Rosemary realized that her sister's hands were still motionless. "You'd best get started again, Susan," she said. Then as much to spur herself as her sister, Rosemary added, "With the threat of Clinton coming up the Hudson, we should hurry even more."

"Which Clinton?" Susan asked with a puzzled frown.

"The British one—Sir Henry Clinton, of course. Certainly you did not think I meant the newly elected governor of our state, George Clinton, or his brother James Clinton, who is a general in our own Continental Army."

The younger girl mumbled, "Henry Clinton, James Clinton, George Clinton—it seems as if York State has as many Clintons as it does apples!"

Rosemary laughed at her sister's exaggeration, then became serious. "Only one Clinton too many," she said. "The one sailing up the Hudson. If the chain at Fort Montgomery doesn't stop him, Sir Henry Clinton will..."

Rosemary's words were cut off in mid-sentence by a shout coming from the nearby farmhouse. As both girls turned in that direction, a woman burst from the door of their home, frantically waving for them to return.

Apples flew in all directions as the two sisters scrambled down the short slope and came to a breathless halt in front of their mother.

"Vaughan's coming! Vaughan's coming!" the woman cried. "With your father and most of the other men away with the militia, we must seek safety elsewhere!"

"Who's Vaughan?" Susan wanted to know.

"Clinton's commander," her mother answered briefly.

"Which Clinton?"

Ignoring her youngest daughter's question, the worried woman's words tumbled out in a rush. "We must move back from the river...out of range of Vaughan's cannon. Women and children are to hide in the forest... Clinton has ordered it..."

"Which Clinton?" Susan repeated.

"Oh, you and your never-ending questions!" Rosemary declared in exasperation. Then seeing that her younger sister was almost in tears, she lowered her voice. "It *is* confusing, Susan, I'll admit. But don't be afraid. I'll explain it all to you just as soon as we do what Clinton has ordered."

"But which..." Susan started to ask, but thought better of it. Instead, she said, "What can I do to help?"

"Go get the cow," her mother directed. "Meanwhile, Rosemary and I will gather up whatever valuables we can carry."

"And hurry, Susan!" Rosemary urged, her face now as pale as her mother's.

As soon as Susan had returned with the cow, the small group set out in a westerly direction. Within minutes they were joined by other settlers whose farms were also located along the west bank of the Hudson River. One of the neighbors offered to take charge of the cattle, saying he would drive them to a safe place. Meanwhile, the women and children were to go as fast as they could to the other side of Illinois Mountain.

There was only a rough trail to follow, and the first part of the ascent was steep. So it wasn't until they stopped to rest for a few moments in a wooded glade halfway up the mountain that Rosemary had enough breath to talk to her sister. Only then did Susan fully comprehend the reason for their flight.

Ever since the Revolution began a little over a year ago in 1776, the British had tried to gain control of the Hudson River. The British felt that if they could accomplish this, they would soon win out over the rebels and end the war. With this in mind, a three-pronged advance was planned. British General John Burgoyne was to move south from Lake George along the upper Hudson Valley. Meanwhile, Colonel Barry St. Leger would lead his soldiers east along the Mohawk Valley to the Hudson. At the same time, Sir Henry Clinton was to advance north up the Hudson from New York City. When the three forces met, the Hudson River would be in the hands of the British.

In an attempt to stop the British ships from moving northward, a huge chain had been strung across the Hudson from Fort Montgomery to Anthony's Nose on the east bank of the river. Somehow Sir Henry Clinton's forces, with Vaughan in command, had broken through the chain. The British had attacked Fort Montgomery and Fort Clinton, and were now sailing upriver, bombarding the shoreline as they came.

"So now you know which Clinton we mean," Rosemary concluded, as the small group of settlers prepared to start out again.

Susan shivered, even though she was perspiring from the long climb up the face of Illinois Mountain. Her mother was busy helping one of the other women with a set of year-old twins, and Susan knew she should not bother her. However, there was one more question she just had to ask. So she turned again to Rosemary.

"Where... where can we go that we'll be safe?" Despite her attempt to appear brave, Susan's voice quavered as she said this.

Rosemary had just picked up the heavy bundle of household items wrapped up in a quilt, but she set it down again. Taking her younger sister in her arms, she soothed, "Don't worry, Susan. We're going to the Rock House. The British will never find us there."

Encouraged by Rosemary's assurances, Susan once more started up the mountain. She was still afraid, but part of the fear had been replaced by thoughts of their destination. The Rock House—the name intrigued her. Anxious to see it, she increased her pace, even though her legs were now tired from climbing.

Eventually the narrow trail they followed began to slope downward, and before long the weary group of women and children found themselves in a secluded, boulder-strewn valley on the western slope of the mountain.

Before them, like a huge gray fortress, stood the Rock House. Susan gasped at its size, then gasped again when Rosemary told her it was made up of two massive boulders which had fallen from the mountain long ago.

One boulder had come to rest leaning against the side of the other, with the result that a capacious, cave-like shelter had been formed between the two.

As the women went about arranging their belongings inside the Rock House, the children silently crowded around them, unwilling to be separated from their mothers by any more than a few feet. However, an hour's rest, plus some of the cold beef and bread the women had brought along, restored the youngsters' spirits. One by one they left the confines of the Rock House to play outside in the October sunshine. All of them, that is, but Susan.

"Come on, Susan," Rosemary urged. "Let's go outside. Why, if I didn't know any better, I'd think it was a picnic we're having."

"Some picnic," Susan said gloomily, "with the enemy just a few miles away."

Realizing that Susan was still disturbed over the British threat, Rosemary quickly pointed out, "We don't know whether the British even landed. They may have continued on upriver. Coming here was only a precaution."

When the nine-year-old girl still didn't respond, Rosemary decided that a little bit of good-natured teasing might be just the medicine her sister needed.

"I really don't see why you're so gloomy," Rosemary began. "After all, you got your wish, didn't you?"

"My wish?" the puzzled girl echoed.

"Wasn't it you who wanted a day away from the apples?" Rosemary reminded her with a grin.

The beginnings of a smile turned up the corners of Susan's mouth as she answered, "Well, maybe I did hope to have a day off, but I certainly didn't expect it would be the British who gave it to me!"

"Think of it as a gift," Rosemary suggested. "A gift from the enemy."

Susan began to chuckle at the thought. "That would be something," she said. "A gift from Clinton!"

"Which Clinton?" Rosemary teased, sounding just

THE ROCK HOUSE CAVE

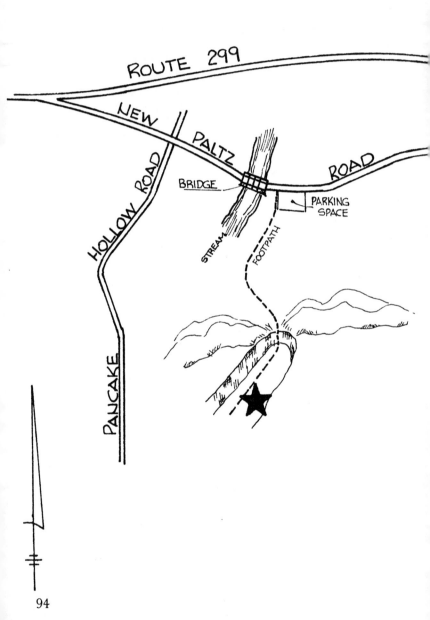

like Susan. Then Rosemary raced out of the Rock House, with her laughing sister hot on her heels.

The British did not land near the Rock House that day. Though they bombarded the west bank of the Hudson with cannonfire from their ships, their objective was Kingston (then the state capital) farther to the north.

Word soon came to those hiding in the Rock House that it was safe to return to their homes, and they left their mountain refuge. The Rock House was not forgotten, however. In the two centuries that have elapsed since it sheltered the women and children of the New Paltz-Highland area, this boulder-built cave has been a popular picnicking site for all those who like to combine the beauty of nature with the lure of history.

How to Get There

The Rock House, south of New Paltz Road, between New Paltz and Highland, New York. From its intersection with IS 87 in New Paltz, go east on Route 299 approximately two and a half miles to the New Paltz Road. Turn right on this road, traveling in a southeasterly direction for about a mile. Just past the intersection of Pancake Hollow Road, you will come to a low bridge with white guard rails, which spans a stream. From the small parking area on the other (eastern) end of the bridge, a trail can be seen leading off to the right (south) towards Illinois Mountain (also known as Mount Refuge). Take this trail (a good one, but steep in places) for about a mile. You will approach the Rock House from the back, but it is easy to spot, as these giant gray boulders stand alone a few yards to the left of the trail. (Approximate walking time: 30 minutes.)

10 Real Caves In Fiction

The morning sun was just warming the head of the Sleeping Lion when James slipped out of the arched front door of Otsego Hall. The young man paused for a moment to gaze north at the golden-tipped rocky prominence, its base still bathed in the swirling mist rising from the lake. Its proper name was Mount Wellington, James reminded himself. But he preferred to call it the Sleeping Lion, just as he preferred rising at dawn to tramp in the woods, rather than waiting to have breakfast with his family as a proper gentleman might do.

Maybe that was the trouble, James admitted to himself as he continued along the lake shore, his dove-gray pants already soaked to the knees by the dew still clinging to every leaf and blade of grass. Maybe there was too much of the woodsman in him to ever be the kind of gentleman his parents expected him to be. Maybe that was why he found it so difficult to concentrate on his studies in a school so far away from his beloved woods.

But why think about that today? he asked himself. He was home on holiday and the sun was shining and the outdoors was his to roam in as he chose. Why spoil it with thoughts of school and being a proper gentleman?

His decision made, James then turned east and began climbing the steep slope to one of his favorite places, a cave overlooking the glimmering expanse of Otsego Lake. From there he could see the village of Cooperstown to the south—a village his pioneering father had established many years ago when the area was still a wilderness.

When the trees were in full foliage, they hid most of the houses from view. At such times, James could look out from his cave and imagine how things had been in those far-off days when the Indians still possessed the land and...

A moving shadow suddenly caught his eye. Startled, James froze in his tracks, until he could determine what was silently moving through the woods. Was it a wildcat? No, now he could see the hunched shoulders of a man quickly retreating down the hill.

Had the man been coming from the cave? If so, what had he been doing there? And who was he anyway? A neighbor would surely have said hello. So it had to be a stranger—or was it?

Nathaniel Shipman! The name flashed into James' mind. And as he continued climbing up to the cave, James recalled the tragic story of the hermit of Cooperstown.

Long before James had been born, Nathaniel Shipman had fought heroically in the French and Indian War. An expert woodsman with close ties to the Mohican tribe, he had later refused to take sides when the Revolutionary War broke out in 1776 and the Mohicans sided with the British. During those perilous times, however, Shipman's neutrality was unacceptable to his neighbors. Taking the law into their own hands, they tarred and feathered the hapless woodsman. Soon after, Shipman disappeared from his home in Hoosick Falls.

For the next twenty-six years, Nathaniel Shipman lived the life of a hermit near the shores of Otsego Lake, north of Cooperstown. Eventually Judge William Cooper (James' father) heard about Shipman and sent his son-in-law, John Ryan, to find the missing man.

Ryan brought Shipman back to Hoosick Falls but the old woodsman had never forgiven the people who

tarred and feathered him. Therefore, he often returned to Cooperstown, where he had spent so many lonely years.

Maybe it had been Nathaniel Shipman who had slipped off through the woods. The idea appealed to James, who looked around the cave, trying to imagine the old hermit living in its rocky confines. Yes, it was possible, he decided. There was also the possibility that at one time Indians had used the cave, for it was a natural fortress as well as an ideal lookout post.

As he sat there in the cave, young James' vivid imagination created scenes of what might have occurred there in bygone days. And though he would never know whether Nathaniel Shipman had used this as a haven, the cave would play a prominent part in one of the books James later wrote. For the full name of this young man was James Fenimore Cooper, who won lasting fame for his Leatherstocking tales.

Comprising five novels in all, the Leatherstocking tales include such classics as *The Last of the Mohicans* and *The Deerslayer.* However, it was in the very first one, *The Pioneers,* that the cave was featured.

It is probable, too, that Nathaniel Shipman at least partially served as the model for one of the best-loved characters in all of Cooper's fiction—the expert woodsman, Natty Bumppo (also known as Hawkeye, Leatherstocking, the Pathfinder and La Longue Carabine).

Although it can be argued that Cooper also had Daniel Boone in mind when he created Natty Bumppo, anyone who learns the tragic story of Nathaniel Shipman cannot help but see similarities between the old hermit and the fictional Natty. There are others who disagree, maintaining that Cooper patterned Natty Bumppo after a leather-clad woodsman named David Shipman (no relation to Nathaniel), who used to supply the Cooper family with deer and bear meat.

Since Cooper himself never said who was the model for Natty Bumppo, the controversy has never been resolved. Perhaps he combined characteristics of all three real-life woodsmen to create the unforgettable hero of the Leatherstocking tales.

Fortunately, there is no such controversy over the cave Natty Bumppo used, for Cooper described it vividly in *The Pioneers,* even to the "terrace" on which the heroine stood during a forest fire. The novelist did not give the cave a name, but it has since become known as Natty Bumppo's Cave, and is located only a short distance from where Cooper lived as a boy.

It is a small cave, but it is as impressive in fact as it is in fiction. Therefore, it is no wonder that James Fenimore Cooper, who had an eye for the unusual, chose it as the setting for some of the most exciting scenes in *The Pioneers.* Nor is it surprising that people still visit the dark recesses on a hill high above the beautiful lake which we call Otsego, but which Cooper called Glimmerglass.

There is another cave, farther to the northeast, which James Fenimore Cooper used as the scene for the climax of what is probably the most famous of his novels, *The Last of the Mohicans.* Those who have read the story, or have seen the televised version of it, will remember the cave. It is the one through which Uncas pursued Magua and the captured Cora, and above which the three of them were to meet their death.

James Fenimore Cooper first visited this cave around 1825, when an innkeeper near Glens Falls told the novelist and his traveling companion, Lord Derby (later Prime Minister of England), about its existence on the bank of the nearby Hudson River. Cooper was so impressed by its beauty that he gave this cave—eroded out of the bedrock by the action of the Hudson's water—an important place in his very next novel.

The spot immediately became a popular attraction for tourists, and in 1913 a spiral staircase was erected for easy access to the cave. In time, however, the river continued to eat away at the rocks surrounding the cave. The high water of spring deposited much debris at the mouth of the

Natty Bumppo's Cave

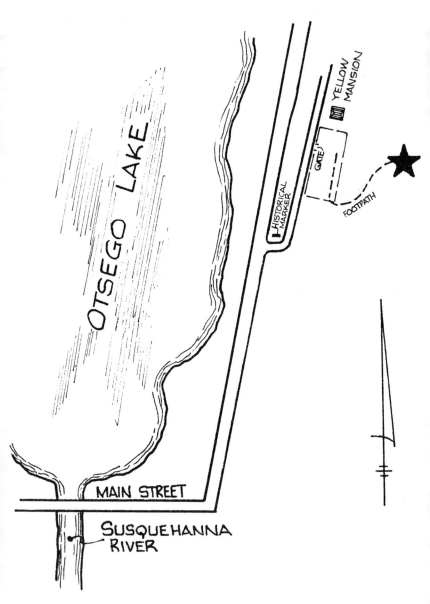

OTSEGO LAKE

YELLOW MANSION

GATE

HISTORICAL MARKER

FOOTPATH

MAIN STREET

SUSQUEHANNA RIVER

COOPERSTOWN

cave and marred the loveliness Cooper had so admired.

In 1959, when the bridge between Glens Falls and South Glens Falls was rebuilt, the spiral staircase was closed off and later removed entirely. The cave is still there and can be easily viewed from the eastern end of the bridge. However, it is now practically inaccessible to visitors, because it is considered hazardous and unsafe by the State of New York, which presently owns the land surrounding it. It can only be hoped that someday the State will restore this historic site for the enjoyment of present and future generations.

How to Get There

Natty Bumppo's Cave, off East Lake Drive, north of Cooperstown, New York. Go north from the village of Cooperstown on the unmarked, narrow but paved road that follows the eastern shore of Otsego Lake. About a mile from the village there is a historical marker (with the name of "Bumppo" misspelled, by the way) on the right-hand side of the road. Turn into the dirt road which leads up the hill from the marker. On your right, you will soon see a large pasture enclosed by a rail fence with a white gate. On the north end of the pasture is a handsome chalet-style mansion, where permission should be obtained for visiting the cave. Go through the white gate and cross the pasture to where it meets the heavily forested hill. Paralleling the hill, a footpath leads to the southeastern corner of the pasture, where the trail continues up the hill. A stiff climb along this trail will bring you to the entrance of the cave. (Approximate walking time: 15 minutes from pasture gate.)

11 Niagara's Pit of the Evil Spirit

Though he was dressed in clothing suitable for the wilderness trek to Lake Ontario, Robert Cavelier Sieur de La Salle looked every inch the French aristocrat he was. Yet even this experienced traveler paused in wonder as he looked down at the gaping hole in the cliff which bordered the thundering Niagara River.

His Indian guide was equally impressed, yet there was more fear than interest in his dark eyes as he placed a restraining hand on the arm of the French explorer.

"Go no closer," Garonkouthie advised. "That is the home of the Evil Spirit."

"Evil Spirit!" La Salle echoed, and was about to scoff at the superstition until he saw the grim expression on his companion's face. "Tell me about this Evil Spirit," he urged instead.

His eyes still on the cavern below them, the Seneca guide began, "Ages and ages of prosperity and happiness to the red man had passed from the time of his creation. The Great Spirit loved his red children and gave them this country for their sole use and enjoyment." The Indian sighed as he pointed downriver to the great cataract that would in later days be called Niagara Falls. Then he resumed his story.

"So it would have continued forever, if the Great Falls of Onguiaahra, whose thunder we now hear so plainly, had continued near the spot where your canoe landed."

La Salle looked up the river in amazement. Could it be that this giant cataract had once entered the river at some other place? It seemed impossible, but Garonkouthie was far too serious for La Salle to question his words.

"But the red man became bad," the Seneca continued, "and the Great Spirit was angered by the red man's war parties. The rocks began to fall off the banks of the river and the ledge of the falls. There were great storms, and scarcely a moon passed that some change did not occur."

The guide pointed to a deep ravine in the river bank. "It was here that the mighty river once flowed. It filled the empty chasm you now see before you, covering over the cave down below where the Evil Spirit lived. When the rocks fell, the river no longer filled the chasm, and the Evil Spirit was freed from the Devil's Hole."

"Devil's Hole, eh?" La Salle murmured, but the guide was intent on his tale and did not hear him.

"Noises of thunder, shrieks and groans were often heard from this dark den. The young men of the tribe became curious, and one of them decided to explore the cave at the bottom of the chasm. Armed for battle, he descended with much difficulty, and disappeared into the Devil's Hole. We never saw him again.

"Soon after that, word came that pale-faced men, in vast canoes which could each carry an army, had landed on the shore of the great sea to the east. But since they were far away, we thought little of it.

"Time passed, and another of our young men descended into the Devil's Hole. He returned in a few hours, a raving maniac. His hair, which had been black and glossy as a raven, had become as white as snow.

"Then came word that still other pale-faced men had been seen sailing west on the river that leads to the great sea. Our fathers decided that the strangers had come because the two young men had gone down into the

Devil's Hole. They were convinced that the Evil Spirit lived in this deep dark hole, and that the fate of our people depended upon his not being disturbed."

La Salle nodded slowly, but Garonkouthie sensed that the Frenchman was not convinced. "You are thinking of going into the Devil's Hole," the Seneca rightly guessed. "But I must warn you that whoever disturbs the Evil Spirit must pay the penalty, as did the two braves who entered it long years ago."

Despite himself, La Salle shivered. Turning away from the Devil's Hole, he told the Seneca, "I will respect the beliefs of your people, Garonkouthie. I will not explore the cavern."

Satisfied, the Indian returned with La Salle to their camp near the mouth of the Niagara River. But La Salle could not stop thinking of the Devil's Hole, and before two days had passed he returned alone to the precipice above the cave. Challenge had won out over caution, and he descended into the ravine.

As soon as he did, he heard what seemed to be a human voice coming from the mouth of the cave. Once inside, the voice was stronger, and the Frenchman could make out words. The voice spoke in the Iroquois language, and it warned him against his proposed journey to the west.

"Return to your home in Canada," the voice told him. "And wealth, honors and a long life of usefulness shall be yours. Then when death comes, generations of your descendants shall follow you to your grave, and history shall transmit your name to posterity as the successful founder of a great empire."

The voice paused, as if to give La Salle time to weigh the advantages of returning to Canada. Then it predicted the dire alternative:

"Proceed to the west, and although gleams of hope may, at times, shine in your path, ingratitude and disappointment will be sure to meet and follow you. Finally, a treacherous murder shall end your days in a place remote from human habitation, without the shelter of even a wigwam of a friendly red man. The eagles of the desert shall strip the flesh from your bones which shall lay bleaching under a tropical sun, unburied and unprotected by the Cross you now so devoutly cherish."

Horrified, La Salle did not want to hear any more and scrambled out of the cave to hurry back to his camp. There he was to find that some of his men had deserted him to return to Montreal. Whether or not he considered this to be a sign that the dire prophecy was already coming to pass, La Salle did not heed the mysterious voice of the Devil's Hole, and he resumed his journey to the west.

In time, La Salle was to experience each and every one of the predictions made at the Devil's Hole. Financial failure, mutiny, enemies in government, desertion, sickness, false friends, shipwreck — all of these were to plague him until finally, in 1687, he was assassinated by his own men in the wilderness "remote from human habitation."

La Salle's death did not bring about the end of unfortunate events associated with the cave called the Devil's Hole. The strange noises that emanated from its depths continued to mystify and strike fear in the hearts of most men who chanced to hear its ominous "thunderings of doom."

However, the next time the Devil's Hole was involved in misfortune, it was not through any mysterious voice coming from the cave. Rather, it was real live Senecas who raised their voices in the war cries that initiated the Devil's Hole Massacre of 1763.

Four years earlier, in 1759, the British and French had fought the battle of La Belle Famille, three miles south of Fort Niagara. At its conclusion, the French were defeated and the British took over the area.

Due to the Falls and the turbulent water, the Niagara River was not navigable in its center portion. Therefore, the French had used Seneca Indians to carry goods overland from the Lake Erie end of the Niagara River to where it joined Lake Ontario. This route was called the Niagara Portage.

When the British took over, they decided that

animal power would be more economical than Indian power, and so they built a road to accommodate the wagon trains they planned to use instead of the Senecas.

By September 1763 the road was completed, and on the fourteenth day of that month the first wagon train set out under the direction of wagonmaster John Stedman.

The convoy had just come abreast of the infamous Devil's Hole when shrill cries shredded the late summer air. Hundreds of Senecas—enraged over losing their portaging jobs—descended on the helpless wagon train.

Within minutes, wagons and animals, along with their drivers, had been hurled over the rim of the gorge, the cries of the dying mingling with the triumphant shouts of the Senecas.

The only survivors were wagonmaster John Stedman, who escaped on horseback, and a drummer boy named Matthews, who had jumped over the edge to escape the marauding Indians. Luckily, the boy landed in a tree, where he remained until the Indians rode off.

When the carnage was reported to the British troops stationed at nearby Lewiston, two companies set out to apprehend the Indians. But the Senecas had set up still another ambush, and the sixty-nine British soldiers soon joined the twenty-four civilians who had perished.

As if that bloodbath had satisfied the Evil Spirit supposedly lodged within the Devil's Hole, there have been no more tragedies associated with it. Yet the strange sounds which sometimes come from its depths have persisted down through the centuries, and even today there are superstitious people who refuse to descend the stone stairs that lead to its mouth.

The sounds of the cave probably are the result of a combination of wind and the tumbling Niagara nearby, producing echoes against the scoured walls of the Devil's Hole. Not so easily explained, however, is the meaning of the peculiar excavations to be found inside the cave. Scientists have determined these excavations to be the work of some prehistoric people.

Strangely enough, scientists have also given some

DEVIL'S HOLE CAVE

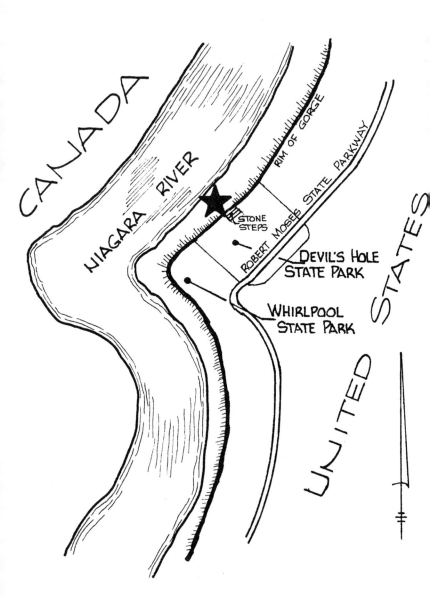

CANADA

NIAGARA RIVER

RIM OF GORGE

ROBERT MOSES STATE PARKWAY

STONE STEPS

DEVIL'S HOLE STATE PARK

WHIRLPOOL STATE PARK

UNITED STATES

credence to part of the Seneca legend concerning the Devil's Hole. Though the great cataract itself never descended at this point, at some time after the Ice Age, an arm of the Niagara River did indeed form the perpendicular cuts in the rock above the cave.

As for the Evil Spirit being allowed to escape, there is a giant rock called Ambush Boulder near the entrance of the cave which could have served to plug up the entrance until the time when the "rocks began to fall off."

The changes described in the Seneca legend have not been limited to the past, and as recently as 1954 a tremendous rock slide tumbled tons of boulders from the underlying ledge of the American Falls. But the Devil's Hole remains much the same as it was in the days when La Salle defied the voice that still occasionally thunders from its depths.

How to Get There

Devil's Hole Cave, Devil's Hole State Park, Niagara Falls, New York. From the center of the city of Niagara Falls, take the Robert Moses State Parkway north to the small (only 42 acres) Devil's Hole State Park. This is situated on the rim of the gorge. Follow the path along the top of the gorge until you come to the Devil's Pulpit. Here a stone stairway descends down to the river level and the cave. (Approximate walking time: 5 minutes from the rim of the gorge.)

12 Strange Partnership– The Vengeance of Tom Quick and Cahoonzie

Standing with apparent defiance before the two white men, the Indian boy hoped that his face did not reveal the fear he felt. By keeping his legs ramrod-stiff, he could quell the trembling in his knees. However, there was nothing he could do to calm the apprehensive twitch that played along the edge of his tightly clamped jaw.

"He's got spirit, eh?" one of the white men observed with a touch of admiration in his voice.

The other man nodded as he studied the small figure before them. "Aye, he has that, Lord Henry," he grudgingly conceded.

"Plus a fair share of intelligence, if I'm not mistaken," the first man continued.

"An intelligent savage! Bah! What may appear to you as intelligence is only the cunning of a wild animal— nothing more."

Getting up from his chair, Lord Henry went over to the Indian boy. His shoulder flinched when the older man placed his hand on it, yet the hand remained there in a way that was more comforting that restraining. And despite his fear, the boy no longer trembled.

"Only the cunning of a wild animal?" Lord Henry echoed the other man's words. "Did you ever see a wild animal cultivate crops or make effective medicines from wild plants?" Shaking his head decisively, he went on, "No, Will, you are wrong. You are forgetting that the early colonists would never have survived without the help and knowledge of these so-called savages."

"That was a long time ago—before King Philip's War, before the Pequot War and before this savage's people burned out the village where my wife and children died!"

Lord Henry sighed. "And so, we murdered some of his people in return." Then sadly he asked, "Must this hate go on forever?"

The Indian's glance darted from one bearded man to the other. Although he did not understand each and every word that was said, he knew a little of the white man's language. It had been taught to him by his uncle who occasionally bartered with the outlying settlements—that is, before his uncle had been killed in the recent conflict.

The memory of his uncle's death and his own capture caused the boy's hatred to flare anew. He could barely concentrate on what the white man—the one called Lord Henry—was saying to him.

"Tell me your name," Lord Henry was urging. Pointing to himself, he went on, "I am Henry." Then more slowly, "Hen-ry."

The man's finger poked at the boy's bare chest, and before he could remember that he did not want to answer this enemy, the boy said, "Cahoonzie. I am Cahoonzie."

Lord Henry smiled suddenly. "Well, well. Cahoonzie, is it? Now if we..."

"Begging your pardon, Lord Henry," Will interrupted. "What do you intend doing with this savage?"

"Not savage, Will. His name is Cahoonzie, and I'll thank you to call him that."

There was an exasperated snort, but Will knew better than to argue with his employer. So he remained silent, glaring at the Indian boy, who returned the challenge with dark eyes flashing.

Lord Henry sighed wearily, but his voice was determined when he said, "I'm taking Cahoonzie back with us to England."

"What?"

"I'm going to educate the boy, and. . ."

"Educate a savage?"

"I'll wager that as soon as he learns our language he will be an apt scholar," Lord Henry continued, ignoring Will's outburst. "In any event, Will, did it ever occur to you what an advantage an educated Indian might be? He could act as an intermediary — a sort of representative — in our trading ventures with the various tribes."

Will's mouth opened wide in surprise, and for a moment he considered Lord Henry's startling plan for Cahoonzie's future. Then Will shook his head slowly. "Mark my words, Lord Henry. At the first opportunity, your educated Indian will revert to being a savage — and you may deeply regret your experiment."

"We'll see, Will. We'll see," Lord Henry murmured.

In a way, both men would be proven right. Cahoonzie was, indeed, an apt scholar, and his stay in England provided him with an education that few boys could hope to receive in the latter half of the 18th Century.

Yet as his ship approached New York harbor many years later, the Indian was deeply troubled. Now a man, Cahoonzie was returning to America to represent a group of merchants interested in obtaining furs from the Indians.

The ship had dropped anchor in the bay, waiting for daylight before attempting to dock. On deck, Cahoonzie stared at the lights of the city, which shined in the night like a giant swarm of fireflies. Each light meant a house — a house with confining walls — white men's walls.

Turning away, Cahoonzie gazed at those dark patches where no lights punctured the night. At the line where the blackness of the land met the lesser darkness of the sky, the Indian could see the vague silhouettes of trees.

Somewhere far beyond those trees was the village where he had been born. Somewhere beyond those trees were his people. Somewhere. . .

The watchman at the helm of the ship heard the splash as Cahoonzie's slim form knifed into the water. The watchman listened for a moment, then decided it had been only the splash of some surfacing fish. Therefore, he did not see the lone figure swimming toward the dark line of trees in the distance.

For many days Cahoonzie traveled toward the village of his people, learning again the ways of the woods which he had almost forgotten during his many years in England. He imagined the excitement his return would cause, and, thus, his anticipation intensified with every mile he covered. But there was no excitement—there was nothing but a numbing grief that would soon turn into flaming hatred.

For when Cahoonzie emerged in the clearing which had held the lodges of his people, he found only desolation. The entire village had been destroyed by a band of warring Delawares. And it was there, among the tumbled lodgepoles and the unburied dead, that Cahoonzie swore he would exact a bloody vengeance on all members of the Delaware tribe.

Unknown to Cahoonzie at this time, there was another man—a white man—who had sworn a similar oath. That man was Tom Quick.

Tom Quick was born in 1736 near Milford, Pennsylvania. Life was not easy for a farmer on what was then considered the frontier, and by the time Tom was twenty, he was an experienced woodsman and hunter as well as a farmer.

It was during the winter of 1756 that Tom and his father were crossing the ice-bound Delaware River on their way to a nearby mill. Suddenly a musket shot cracked the stillness of the frigid afternoon air, and Thomas Quick Sr. fell to the ice mortally wounded.

His own musket cocked and ready, young Tom searched the shoreline with his eyes, only to see that the attackers were already out of firing range and fleeing into the woods. They were not so far away, however, that Tom could not make out who they were.

A strangled cry erupted from his throat as he bent

over the bleeding body of his father. The attackers had been supposedly *friendly* Indians, well known to the Quick family!

There was no time for Tom to consider that the land of these former friends had been taken away from them by the white men. Tom only knew they had shot his father, whose life was now ebbing away on the crimson-stained ice of the Delaware.

Just before Tom Sr. died, he made his son promise to flee east into New Jersey until the Indian uprising had been quelled. Therefore, when the older man breathed his last, young Tom set out to keep his promise. He also made a vow that he would annihilate at least one hundred Indians to avenge the death of his father.

During the next forty years, Tom Quick was to fulfill his bloodthirsty vow, and shortly before his death in 1796 he even managed to track down Muskwick, the Indian who had slain his father. Prior to this, however, Tom Quick met the renegade Cahoonzie and the two decided to join forces.

It was this strange partnership that resulted in what was perhaps the most daring and unusual ambush ever staged in that part of the country.

A few miles to the west of Port Jervis, New York, looming high above the curving Delaware River, is an awesome rock formation called the Hawk's Nest. Its perpendicular stone face has been carved by eons of nature's sculptors into deep furrows, crevices and clefts. It made an ideal home for the hawks which roosted there and gave the mountain its name.

It is also ideal for hunters — be they hunters of man or beast. For from the brow of the Hawk's Nest, there is an excellent view of the countryside. The highest point in the Shawangunk range can be seen to the northeast, while the Catskill Mountains gently rise to the clouds in the north. A third range, the coal-rich Carbon Mountains, rise to the northwest and provided a rocky fortress in which Tom Quick was able to establish one of his notorious ambush caves.

The Hawk's Nest itself was another site, with its

cave-like structure called the Lifting Rocks. This curious formation consists of three stone pillars which rise about five feet from the ground and support huge rocks estimated to weigh from 30 to 100 tons. Since the pillars are an equal distance apart, it appears as if they were set there on purpose, rather than being some geological freak of nature caused by a glacier which traveled over the area during the Ice Age.

Because the cavity formed by the Lifting Rocks is small and narrow, it is doubtful that Tom Quick and Cahoonzie ever relied on it as a shelter. The use they put to it was much more terrible.

The two partners were camped on Hawk's Nest one day when they saw a war party of Delaware Indians in the valley below. Unaware of the eyes that watched them, the Indians made their camp on the bank of the river nearest the mountain. They then went off to fish.

Above them, Tom Quick and Cahoonzie hurriedly planned an attack. First, they smeared the Lifting Rocks with pitch. Then the two avengers gathered dried wood, which they stuffed inside the small cave and around the pillars of the Lifting Rocks.

When this was accomplished, Tom Quick stealthily made his way down the mountain, skirting the party of Delawares who had by now returned to their camp. Choosing a spot between them and the river, Tom Quick waited for a signal from Cahoonzie. Within minutes a huge column of pitchy smoke came from the fire Cahoonzie had ignited at the Lifting Rocks. This was Tom's signal.

While the attention of the Delawares was fixed on the inferno high above them, Tom Quick set another fire. This, in effect, cut off the Indians' retreat to the river. The flames were soon rampaging through the dry underbrush, alerting the Delawares to the danger.

Just as they prepared to escape by climbing up the mountain, a huge boulder came crashing down toward them. Using the Lifting Rocks as an "oven," Cahoonzie had heated the boulder until it was red-hot. Then he sent it hurtling over the rim of the Hawk's Nest, setting fire to the underbrush as it rolled down. The Delawares were thus trapped between the two forest fires and the entire party perished, without Tom Quick or Cahoonzie firing a shot.

It is relatively easy to reach the crest of Hawk's Nest Mountain. However, the Lifting Rocks, on private land—permission required) are in a precipitous location, and should not be visited by any except experienced rock climbers. Even then, the crumbling rock, whose many eroded crevices serve as homes for copperheads as well as hawks, gives no guarantee of secure passage.

On the other hand, Tom Quick's Cave, just across the river, is easily accessible as well as safe. While not the site of such a spectacular ambush as the one staged at the Lifting Rocks, this small rock shelter still served as a "base of operations" during Tom Quick's long career as an Indian fighter. The cave is on the Pennsylvania side of the Delaware, but because it is so much a part of the Tom Quick story and so close to Lifting Rocks, it has been included here.

How to Get There

Tom Quick's Cave, about two miles southeast of Pond Eddy, New York. Go north from Port Jervis on Route 97 (Hawk's Nest Road). Stop at one of the small roadside parking areas to look up at the Hawk's Nest. (During the months when the foliage is not dense, the Lifting Rocks can be seen high upon Hawk's Nest.) Proceed along this scenic drive to Pond Eddy. Here you make a left turn across the narrow bridge spanning the Delaware River. Make another left turn at the end of the bridge onto a nar-

THE LIFTING ROCKS AND TOM QUICK'S CAVE

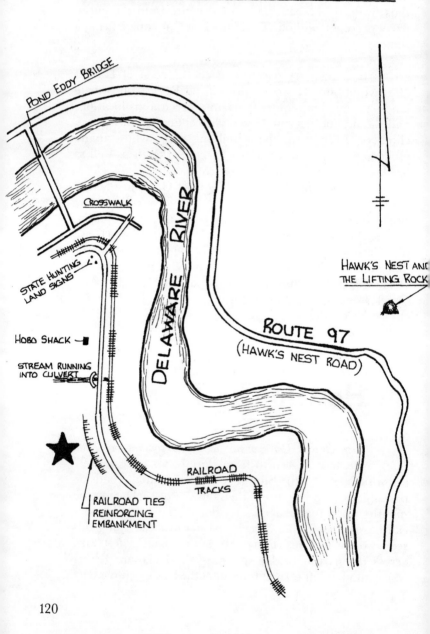

POND EDDY BRIDGE

CROSSWALK

DELAWARE RIVER

HAWK'S NEST AND THE LIFTING ROCK

STATE HUNTING LAND SIGNS

ROUTE 97
(HAWK'S NEST ROAD)

HOBO SHACK

STREAM RUNNING INTO CULVERT

★

RAILROAD TRACKS

RAILROAD TIES REINFORCING EMBANKMENT

row road which runs parallel to the river on your left. Continue down this road until you come to a railroad crossing on your right. (The road you are on becomes a private road after this point.) Cross the railroad tracks. On the other side, you will see signs on the trees at the edge of the woods proclaiming this to be state hunting land.

Turn left (east) down the wide path running parallel to the railroad tracks. You will pass an old hobo shack on your right, and then a stream which runs down the hill (again on your right) into a culvert under the tracks. About 100 yards farther on, there is an embankment on your right which has been reinforced by old railroad ties. Make a right turn, climb the embankment and proceed up the hill about 150 feet to the ledge of rock (the only one in the immediate vicinity) at the base of which you will see Tom Quick's Cave. (Approximate walking time: 40 minutes from Pond Eddy bridge.)

13 Where Millard Fillmore Roamed

The storm had come up from nowhere—or so it seemed to the frightened girl who now raced through the woods.

Jenny paused when she came to a clearing. Looking up through the break in the trees overhead, she could see the churning gray-black clouds rumbling angrily as they bumped into one another. They were so thick that the bright afternoon was quickly being smothered by gloomy darkness.

Could she make it home before the storm broke? Would she be able to get out of the woods before the searing bolts of lightning sent down their prongs of death?

Jenny shuddered, her gasping breath searing her throat just as the lightning had seared her brother Tad that terrible day five years ago.

Jenny had been only six years old when it happened, but she could still remember what Tad had looked like when they found him. His lifeless body had been pinned under a huge oak tree that had been split down the middle by the lightning.

Since that time Jenny was terrified of storms—so terrified that at the first clap of thunder she would hurry inside the farmhouse, in which she lived, to hide under her bed. At first her parents had tolerated her fear and tried to soothe her whenever a storm sent her scurrying for a hiding place. But lately they had been less patient, especially her father. He had ordered her to come out from under the bed the last time a storm had raged over Lake Owasco to the north.

"Why, that storm's miles away from here," he had said. "Anyway, Jenny, you can't go on hiding for the rest of your life."

Jenny had done as he ordered, but that did not mean she was any less afraid.

Maybe she really was an honest-to-goodness "scairdy cat," as her younger brother Ralph had taunted so many times. She didn't want to be, but she just couldn't help it. Ralph had been only a baby in 1846 when Tad died. Maybe if Ralph had seen what happened he wouldn't be so quick to call her that.

Another clap of thunder—louder than the ones before—made Jenny look up at the sky again. Just as she did so, a many-pronged fork of lightning hurtled through the sky.

How many seconds had elapsed between the thunder and the lightning? Jenny had not counted, but she knew there had been only a very brief interval. That meant the storm was directly overhead—that the lightning would be coming down right on top of her!

Panic surged through the girl as heavy drops of rain began to filter through the leaves overhead. What could she do? There were trees all around—trees that attracted lightning. She must not stand beneath them. But home was over a mile away. There was no time to get there!

Another ear-splitting crack of thunder was followed almost immediately by a jagged bolt of lightning. For a second the darkness of the forest turned into blinding white light. Then it was dark again and a pungent ozone-like smell filled Jenny's lungs.

The terrified girl plunged through the forest, stopping only at the bank of the creek where it tumbled downward at Boulder Falls. Unable to cross here, she would have to follow the creek downstream, past the Cow Shed and. . .

The Cow Shed! Why hadn't she thought of that before? Then Jenny knew why as the words of her brother Ralph sang out in her mind: "Scairdy cat! Scairdy cat! Jenny is a scairdy cat!"

It had happened last summer when they accompanied their father into the woods to hunt for several lost cows.

"They may be up in the Cow Shed," her father had told them. "Sometimes they go in there to escape the heat on a very hot day or when a storm breaks."

"The Cow Shed?" Jenny had questioned.

Her father nodded and said, "It's a cave up the creek a ways, near Boulder Falls."

They had gone upstream to where the creek dashed down over a series of limestone and shale steps. At the base of the steps, yawning darkly in the bright afternoon sunlight, was the mouth of a cave.

When Jenny had lagged behind, her father had urged, "Come on, Jenny. I'll need your help if old Daisy is in there with her calf. You know how balky she can be."

Still Jenny had held back, suddenly fearful of the darkness beneath the limestone cliff.

"Scairdy cat! Scairdy cat!" her brother Ralph had chanted.

"I am not!" Jenny retorted. "It's just that. . .well, I . . ."

"Come on, girl," her father had urged. "If the president of the United States wasn't afraid to go in there as a boy, surely you must not be either."

Jenny had stared up at her father in surprise. "You mean President Fillmore used to live near here?"

"Indeed he did," her father answered. "Some folks say he even carved his initials on one of the walls inside the Cow Shed. Why don't we look for them while we're at it?"

Jenny had the feeling that her father was just using this as an excuse to coax her inside the cave, so she had stayed outside when he entered the shallow chamber. He had not seemed to notice it, though. A few seconds after he entered, his happy voice rang out, "So there you are, Maybelle. And Sunshine too!"

However, Ralph had noticed that Jenny had not followed them inside. And as they drove the cattle home, he kept whispering so only she could hear: "Scairdy cat! Scairdy cat! Jenny is a scairdy cat!"

That was the reason she had not thought of the Cow Shed before now, Jenny realized. But the cave would be safer than being out here under the trees.

Maybe not, Jenny argued with herself. What if some wild animal had sought shelter there just as the cows had done that day? What if she went in there and found a bobcat or a wolf or a . . .

Another javelin of lightning was hurled through the sky. There was a deafening *crack!* Then the earth shook as a giant tree no more than fifty yards away suddenly fell to the ground. Its scorched stump and a spume of smoke were the only clues as to what had caused its death.

Her decision made for her, Jenny clambered over the rocks leading to the Cow Shed. She did not stop until she was inside the cave, vainly trying to see in its inky blackness.

Only now that she was safely away from the lightning did Jenny's thoughts return to what might be *inside* the Cow Shed. Were those eyes peering out at her from the dark depths?

Shivering in her rain-soaked clothes, Jenny pressed her back against the wall of the cave.

"Scairdy cat! Scairdy cat!" Her brother's words chanted in her mind.

"No, I'm not!" her own voice echoed against the damp walls. The sound gave her some reassurance, especially since it had not been answered by some growl farther inside the cave.

"I'm not a scairdy cat!" Jenny repeated, this time with more firmness. But just in case she wasn't alone, she began groping around for rocks that she might use to protect herself.

"It's one thing to be a scairdy cat and another thing to have a healthy fear of danger," she went on, then almost laughed. Why, she was repeating the very same words her father had used that day when he had ordered her to come out from under the bed. They had meant nothing to her then, but now they did. There *was* a difference.

She was still afraid, Jenny admitted, but she had not panicked. She had correctly chosen the lesser of the two dangers—the Cow Shed over the storm outside. And for one last time, Jenny said, "No, I'm not a scairdy cat. Not at all!"

The storm still raged outside, and Jenny's trembling grew worse—not just from fear this time, but also from her wet clothes. Her teeth began to chatter, and Jenny knew she must move around in order to warm up.

It was then that Jenny remembered what her father had said about President Fillmore. Maybe she could find the initials he was said to have carved on the cave wall. It was true she wouldn't be able to see them, but she could feel for them with her hands.

Thus occupied, Jenny lost track of time—and fear—as she slowly examined every crack and crevice. Meanwhile, the thunder came less frequently, and the inky blackness of the cave slowly dissolved into semidarkness.

Just as the first ray of sunlight inched its way into the mouth of the Cow Shed, Jenny heard someone calling her name. Racing to the entrance, she called back, "Here I am. In the Cow Shed!"

Within seconds, her father was there, hugging her in a tight grip that told Jenny how worried he had been.

"I'm all right, Pa—just wet," Jenny assured him. "In fact, President Fillmore kept me company." Seeing her father's raised eyebrows, she hastily explained, "I spent the time looking for the initials he scratched on the wall, but I couldn't find them."

Her father was silent for a moment, then with a

chuckle he told her, "Never could locate them myself. Maybe there never was any to find."

"Maybe," Jenny agreed with a chuckle of her own. "It doesn't really matter now though, does it, Pa?"

His answer was another hug, and together they left the Cow Shed, scrambling down the rocks to where Ralph waited on the bank of the stream. The little boy's eyes were wide with amazement as he saw his sister emerge from the cave.

"You...you mean you stayed in there all...all alone?" he stammered. When Jenny nodded, he added, "Gee, Sis, I would have been scared to death!"

For a brief moment, the words "scairdy cat" flashed through Jenny's mind. Then with a smile, she promptly dismissed them, leaving them behind her forever at the mouth of the Cow Shed.

Unfortunately, not much is known about the early boyhood of Millard Fillmore, the thirteenth president of the United States. We do know, however, that two years before he was born his parents moved from their home in Bennington, Vermont, to Cayuga County, New York. It was there, in a log cabin, that Millard Fillmore was born on January 7, 1800.

Although the land was exceedingly beautiful in the section where they lived, it was not good for farming, and the future president's childhood was one of poverty and privation. In fact, his parents were so poor that, instead of a cradle, their newborn son slept in a maple-sugar trough.

In his autobiographical "Narrative," written in 1871, Millard Fillmore related that as soon as he was old enough he learned the hard life of a farmer. At first his chores were simple ones such as hoeing and weeding. Later he was assigned such tasks as mowing hay, reaping wheat and, eventually, plowing.

The farm chores were never-ending, even in winter, but occasionally he would borrow a rifle and set off to do some hunting, or to fish in a nearby stream. His strict father often cautioned him that "No man ever prospered

Cow Shed Cave

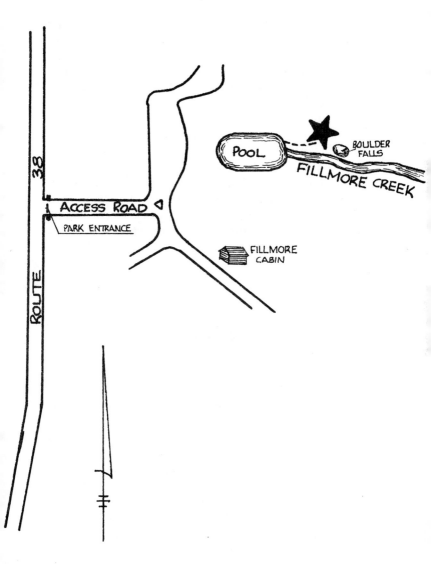

from wasting his time in sporting." But Nathaniel Fillmore had to agree that the results of Millard's "sporting" supplemented the meager family diet. And so the young boy roamed the forest whenever he could.

While Millard Fillmore did not specifically speak of the Cow Shed in his "Narrative," it can be assumed that he knew of its existence, for it was used as a cattle shelter even then. Taking this into consideration, plus the fact that he was an inquisitive boy, always thirsty for knowledge and new experiences, it can be concluded that he surely must have visited the cave, which was only a short distance from the Fillmore cabin.

Today a replica of his boyhood home is even a shorter distance away, having been placed near the entrance to Fillmore Glen State Park, named in honor of this too little-known president. Visitors are welcome to visit the cabin as well as the Cow Shed, and perhaps learn more about our thirteenth president as they view the lovely land where Millard Fillmore once roamed.

How to Get There

Cow Shed Cave, Fillmore Glen State Park, Moravia, New York. Going south from Moravia, on Route 38, turn left (east) at the park entrance and proceed along the access road to the parking lot. (The Fillmore cabin can be seen to the south of the parking lot. It is open daily from May 15 to September 15.) Go east from the parking lot toward the swimming pool. Directly behind the pool you will find an unnamed trail leading east along Fillmore Creek. Proceed along this trail for a short distance to Cow Shed Cave, which is just below Boulder Falls. (Approximate walking time: 15 minutes from parking lot.)

14 Escape From Alpina

Although she worked long hours in the kitchen of Colonel Benton's house, Elizabeth wasn't used to walking far distances. Therefore, by the time she and Henry had traveled a little over two miles, each pebble seemed like a boulder pushing against the thin soles of her shoes. It was especially difficult because Henry avoided the main roads, choosing instead the little-traveled paths and deer trails that looped over the steep hills bordering Mud Lake.

For the last half hour Elizabeth had endured the jabbing pain in her side, but now she was forced to cry out, "Henry, I must rest!"

Her breathless plea immediately halted the young man. "All right, my love," he said gently. But his handsome face bore a worried frown as he looked back over the path they had traveled.

"Surely they would not discover our absence so soon," Elizabeth told him when she had caught her breath. "We will be far away by that time."

Henry nodded. "Aye, that we will," he tried to reassure her. Then he added grimly, "We *must* be."

"If only they would let us marry," Elizabeth sighed.

Before he answered, Henry pulled the girl to her feet. Then he embraced her for a minute and said, "If there was any chance that Colonel Benton would agree to

131

our marriage, I never would have suggested that we run away. But you know what he said — absolutely no wedding so long as we are contracted to serve him."

"Drat him and his contract!" Elizabeth exploded. "Why does he refuse his permission? Doesn't he remember when he fell in love with Princess Caroline and wanted to get married? Joseph Bonaparte did not refuse him — even though Colonel Benton was only the son of a poor North Country physician."

Henry shrugged his wide shoulders. "Joseph Bonaparte had no say in the matter at all, for he went back to Europe long before his daughter Caroline married Colonel Benton. Anyway, I have heard talk that there was no love on the Colonel's part — that he married Princess Caroline only in order to gain her portion of the Bonaparte land and fortune."

"But she's so lovely, with her dark hair and..." Elizabeth's words trailed off as she felt Henry tug at her hand.

"The marriage of Napoleon Bonaparte's niece is no business of ours," the young man asserted. "It is *our* marriage we must be concerned about. So let's be on our way, my love."

Elizabeth followed Henry down the trail that led away from the village of Alpina. Hopefully, they would be well out of the Adirondack foothills before they were discovered missing. Luck was not with them, however, and before they had reached the point where Mud Lake joined Lake Bonaparte, they were being followed.

They were on the northeastern shore opposite Sister Islands when Henry first spotted the riders behind them. Unable to keep his voice steady — for he remembered the flogging he had seen one runaway servant receive — he urged Elizabeth on to greater speed.

"But how can we outdistance men on horseback?" the equally frightened girl cried.

"We can't," Henry answered truthfully, "but we may be able to outwit them."

Elizabeth's lips were just forming the word "How?"

when Henry explained, "One of the older men showed me a cave a few months ago when we were out hunting. It's not far from here—just about a mile to the east, near Green Pond. We can hide there."

"But if others know about the cave, won't they search for us there?" Elizabeth asked.

"I doubt it," Henry replied. "But even if they do, we can hide in one of the inner rooms."

Elizabeth's face turned pale as her memory brought forth all the stories she had ever heard about caves. Visions of ghosts and bears, bobcats and bats flashed into her mind, and she clutched Henry's hand even more tightly than before.

The young man was quick to sense the fear in the girl he loved, and he sought to reassure her. "My love," he began, "please don't be frightened. There's nothing in that cave any more dangerous than a porcupine—and surely you're not afraid of them."

Trying to smile, Elizabeth told him, "Of course not, Henry. In fact, if we're there long enough, I might even make you a porcupine stew!"

Henry laughed outright at the thought of Elizabeth plucking the quills from a fat porcupine and then making a stew from the tough, gamey-tasting meat. Then suddenly he became serious and started off down the fern-bordered deer trail they had been following.

Due to the dense foliage and hilly terrain, they could not determine whether they were still being followed when they reached the mouth of the cave. At first glance, the shallow cavity in the side of the rock face of the hill looked as if it were only an overhang. Further investigation, however, disclosed a low-roofed, narrow passageway at the left side of the shelter.

"In there," Henry pointed, "at the end of the passageway, is a large room maybe 20 feet long and 15 feet wide."

Elizabeth gazed apprehensively at the mouth of the passageway. "But. . .but it's so dark in there, Henry," she couldn't help saying.

Rummaging through the small knapsack he carried, Henry produced two thick candle stubs. "I hadn't thought about the cave when I packed these," he said, "but I'm mighty glad I took them along."

Elizabeth looked at the candles and then at the dark hole that led into the depths of the cave.

"We may not need them at all," Henry said cheerfully. But even as he uttered these words, they could hear the thudding of horses' hoofs on the hill above them.

"Hurry, Elizabeth," Henry urged, already crouching to enter the passageway.

"But Henry, the candle!"

"I'll light it once we get inside."

Elizabeth took a last look at the sunlight reflecting off the still waters of the nearby pond. Then hooking her fingers in the back cross-piece of Henry's suspenders for guidance, she followed him inside.

A short scramble and Elizabeth could feel Henry's bent-over form straightening up.

"Don't stand up all the way, Elizabeth," he cautioned. "The ceiling is just a bit lower than our full height."

Elizabeth waited anxiously until she heard the scratch of a phosphorous match. Then she held her breath as its sputtering flame was held to a candlewick. A quick inspection of the cave relieved Elizabeth's fear somewhat, for not even a porcupine was in residence.

"This is a good hiding place," she had to admit.

But it wasn't. For no sooner had they settled themselves on one of the numerous small rocks that littered the floor than the sound of men shouting could be heard outside.

"Try the passageway into the cave," came the unmistakable voice of the overseer.

"Oh, no!" Elizabeth gasped, when simultaneously with the shouted order the candle seemed to go out.

Henry had not extinguished their only light, however. He had merely moved to the far end of the cave, his sturdy body eclipsing the flame from Elizabeth's view.

Coming back for her, he led her to the spot where he had been. Reaching up with the candle, he illuminated a second smaller chamber about four feet above the level of the place where they now stood.

By some geological quirk, this second room stretched back, with the ceiling of the first room becoming the floor of the second.

Henry managed to keep the candle lighted while they scrambled up into the second chamber. There they huddled breathlessly and listened for sounds from below. Perspiration beaded Elizabeth's now bone-white face, but she did not express her fear.

Proud of his loved one's bravery, Henry drew her close to him, only to feel Elizabeth's body jerk spasmodically when another sound echoed from below.

"There's some kind of opening leading up from the far end of the cave. Think they might be up there?"

"Give it a try," ordered the coarse voice of the overseer.

Henry had pulled Elizabeth over to the entrance of the second room before he explained, "There's a tunnel going up from here to still another chamber."

Elizabeth stood there for only a second. She gazed back down the short passageway that led to the first room, and then she looked up the narrow tunnel rising from the second level.

"There they are!"

The shout from below decided Elizabeth, and she scurried after Henry, who was already crawling up the slope leading into the very bowels of the hill.

They had almost reached the third chamber when the hot wax dripping down the side of the candle caused Henry to drop it. The tiny flame was quickly extinguished in the damp rock dust of the cave floor, and they were suddenly enveloped in pitchy darkness.

"There's water trickling down the side of the tunnel," Elizabeth whispered fearfully.

"Underground spring probably," Henry whispered

back. "The last time I was in here I. . ." His words stopped abruptly.

Even in the darkness Elizabeth could sense his frantic movements as he searched for something in his pockets. Then she heard his frustrated voice telling her, "The matches. . .the matches are *wet!*"

Behind them the voices grew louder and there was the sound of hobnailed boots striking against rock. Their pursuers had reached the second chamber!

Without the candle to light their way, the young lovers knew they dare not go on.

Henry sighed heavily. "I do not think the cave extends any farther than the third chamber," he attempted to console the forlorn girl.

Elizabeth turned toward him, vainly trying to see his face in the darkness. "But if it does go deeper, perhaps *you* could still escape, Henry." He tried to interrupt, but she rushed on, "You are more sure-footed than I am, Henry. You could feel your way in the darkness. You could. . ."

She was finally silenced by his hand over her lips. "No, Elizabeth," he said gently. "I wished to leave Alpina only because of you. What reason would I have to escape if you remain behind?"

"Then I will go with you farther into the cave," came her determined voice.

"No, Elizabeth," he said more firmly. "Without light it is much too dangerous. I could not and would not risk your life. We will return to Alpina and serve out the rest of the time of our contract. Only a few years, then we will be free."

"But what if they flog you for running away?"

"My back is strong," Henry answered simply.

"But what if. . ."

This time Henry's lips silenced Elizabeth's questions. Then together they turned to face the oncoming lights of the men who had cut off their escape from Alpina.

Over the years, there have been many other stories told about Bonaparte's Cave. Some claim that Joseph Bonaparte himself hid there from the Indians, while others relate he used it as a refuge from the French or British. Subsequent investigation by historians has proven that none of these stories is true; those who have studied the history of the area believe that the story which has been told here, concerning the two runaway servants, actually happened.

Joseph Bonaparte, elder brother of Napoleon, was King of Spain for five years until 1813. Not long after that, Napoleon was forced to abdicate as emperor and was exiled to Elba. With financial help from Joseph, Napoleon escaped from Elba on March 1, 1815, only to be defeated at Waterloo three months later.

The gallant Joseph, who resembled his brother, offered to take Napoleon's place at St. Helena where the former emperor was next exiled. This would have allowed Napoleon to escape to the United States, but the defeated emperor refused his brother's offer.

Undaunted, Joseph Bonaparte decided to come to the United States, where he owned thousands of acres of wilderness land in the western foothills of the Adirondacks. (Sensing that his days were numbered as King of Spain, he amassed a fortune in Spanish gold and art treasures while still in that office. He used part of these riches to purchase the land.) His plan was to establish a "New France" in the North Country to which Napoleon might escape at some later date.

The news of Napoleon's death ended such plans forever, and Joseph Bonaparte lost interest in his wilderness acres. Instead, he preferred the more civilized life of such cities as New York, Saratoga, Philadelphia and later Bordentown, New Jersey. During this time Joseph met a lovely young Quaker girl named Annette Savage, and in 1820 a daughter was born, who they named Caroline Charlotte.

Eight years later, Joseph Bonaparte revisited his North Country property. He decided it was fine hunting land and very lovely. So he built a lodge on the eastern shore of the lake which now bears his name, as well as a log house at Natural Bridge to the southwest.

When his daughter Caroline was eighteen, she married Zebulon Howell Benton. Zebulon was a young man who had little to recommend him other than his driving ambition and an exceptional gift for words. After their lavish wedding in 1838, the young couple settled down in the village of Oxbow. Here Benton promptly began to help himself to Caroline's money as well as the land left to her by her father.

Though he dabbled in all kinds of speculative ventures, Benton's main goal was to make a fortune from the rich iron ore which abounded in the land his wife owned. So it was that in the 1840's Colonel Benton (whose title was self-bestowed) became involved with an iron-making company at Alpina. This small community was located near the outlet of Mud Lake, which formed the western arm of Lake Bonaparte.

Colonel Benton's greed, plus his dishonest business dealings, eventually brought about financial ruin to him and his family.

By 1871 all of Caroline's land and money were gone. So was the Colonel, whose love for his wife seemed to have been measured by a dollar sign. Benton went off to live in Alpina, whose blast furnace no longer consumed the rich iron ore he had hoped would make him a millionaire. With the death of its main industry, Alpina died, too, and soon became a ghost town.

Meanwhile, the aging Caroline had moved to Watertown, living with her children, where she eked out a living by giving French lessons. Later she moved to Richfield Springs, near Utica, and it was there she died in 1890.

So ended the story of Caroline Charlotte — daughter of a king and niece of an emperor — who died penniless and almost forgotten on a snowy December day nearly a century ago.

The ghost town of Alpina can still be found on the western shore of Mud Lake. Its huge blast furnace is slowly being crumbled by the ravages of time and the modern-day artillery practice at nearby Camp Drum. These ruins are all that remain, except for the lonely cave farther to the east, where two young people shared a kind of love that their then wealthy mistress was never fortunate enough to possess.

How to Get There

Bonaparte's Cave, near Harrisville, New York. A bridge spans the Oswegatchie River in the village of Harrisville.

BONAPARTE'S CAVE

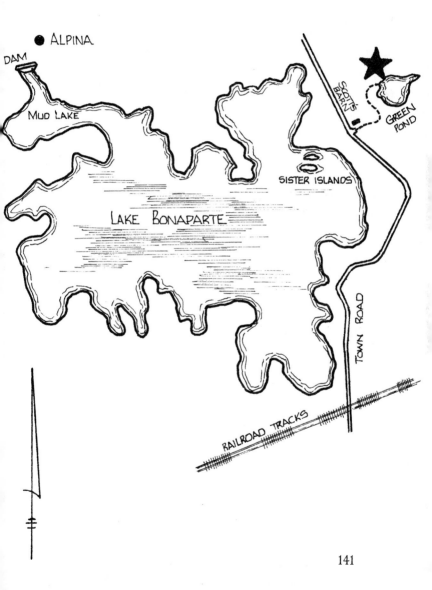

From this bridge go west on Route 3 for one mile until you reach North Shore Road. (There is a sign for Lake Bonaparte.) Make a right turn, and proceed along North Shore Road for half a mile until you come to a crossroads. Make a left turn onto the unmarked town road. You will come to some railroad tracks, which you will cross. Continue along this road for just over a mile until you see a dirt road leading to a pasture. (On the western side — left as you enter — of the pasture, there is an old wooden barn-like structure with "Scott's" marked on its side.)

Follow the path leading through the pasture and into the woods. Keep on this main path for about a third of a mile, being careful not to take any of the narrower, less-traveled trails that branch off from the main path. The path curves up and over a hill, at the base of which you will find Bonaparte's Cave looking out over Green Pond. (Approximate walking time: 15 minutes from the start of the path through the pasture. Although the cave itself is on state land, access to it is through private property. Permission to cross through should first be obtained from Doren Waugh of Harrisville, New York.)

15 North Country Hideout

The heat of the July sun, combined with the dust from the six miles the boy had just walked, made his face almost as dark as an Indian's. Had anyone noticed, the single gold earring in the boy's right ear, plus his homespun clothing, would have shown that he was not one of the hundreds of Indians who had gathered at Johnson Hall. But no one noticed — everyone was too busy talking about the contests that would soon begin.

Each year, Sir William Johnson hosted a field day at the end of which the winner of the most contests would be awarded a bearskin jacket. As Superintendent of Indian Affairs in the Mohawk Valley, the wise Sir William had established these field days in the hope of maintaining friendly relations between the Indians and the many white settlers who had come to the valley.

The festivities were especially important this year because over 600 Indians had converged on Johnson Hall to hold a council. Compounding the problem of settling their many complaints was the growing dissatisfaction of the colonists with the way in which they were ruled by England. Though there had been no open rebellion, Sir William feared that before long blood would be shed.

Eleven-year-old Nick Stoner was not aware of any of these things on that hot July day. All he knew was that

he wanted to win the bearskin jacket and be declared champion of the day.

It would not be easy, the boy had to admit, as he looked over the group which had assembled for the first race. Composed of white men as well as Indians, most of the contestants were much bigger than Nick. There was especially one huge Scottish farm boy who boasted that he would surely be the winner.

Unimpressed, Nick just stared up at the towering Scot. It was not the white settlers that worried him — it was the swift and agile Indians.

Ever since he had come to the Mohawk Valley from New York City, where he had been born, Nick's admiration of the red men had grown. They were the ones who would offer the greatest competition, but the boy was still determined to try.

Ignoring the jibes of those who still laughed at his single gold earring — the gift of an old ship captain who later had been lost at sea — Nick participated in as many of the contests as he could, winning more often than he lost.

Some of the events were fun, such as the sack race and the contest for the worst song. Others were wild and dangerous, like the free-for-all boxing matches and the race where the riders had to sit backwards on their horses. And by the time the footraces began late that afternoon, Nick was a very bruised and weary boy. Yet he would need all the strength he could muster, for footracing was something in which Indians excelled.

Never had Nick run so fast. Never had he competed so hard. Never had he seen such fleet-footed Indians. Sturdy legs churning, his breath coming in shorter and shorter gasps, the dark-haired boy managed to pass each runner until only one was left. Side by side, Nick and the Indian surged across the field.

By now, Nick's breath was like fire in his throat and a sharp pain tore at his chest. He no longer thought of beating the Indian racing alongside him. It was going to be difficult enough to even make it to the finish line, for his legs were numb and he was desperately afraid that he was going to fall.

Each gasping breath was agony. Each step was a mile. But finally Nick staggered over the finish line. As he sprawled face down in the cool grass, the blood was pounding so hard in his ears that he barely heard the cheers proclaiming him the winner.

A short time later, Sir William Johnson placed the coveted bearskin jacket around the shoulders of eleven-year-old Nick Stoner. Even the Indians stood in amazement that anyone so young—and a city-bred lad, at that—could have bested those who had grown up in the forest and were used to such tests of speed and endurance.

So it was that the legend of Nick Stoner began—a legend that is preserved today in such Adirondack place names as Stoner's Island in Canada Lake, Stoner Lakes just north of there, Stoner's Cave near Cranberry Lake, as well as the Stoner Monument at Caroga Lake.

After his victory at Johnson Hall, Nick returned to help on his father's farm which was located about six miles from Johnstown. In his spare time, he continued to wander through the forest. Each day he learned something more about the rich resources and beauty of the Adirondack wilderness.

However, these peaceful days did not last long. The bloodshed Sir William had feared was soon a reality called the Revolutionary War. And in 1777, Nick and his brother John marched off to join the Americans fighting for their liberty. As soon as Henry Stoner had moved the rest of the family to the safety of Johnstown, he joined his sons as a soldier.

Many a river ran red with blood that year—some of it was Nick's; some of it was the blood of his best friend, who gave his own life to save Nick's at Saratoga; and some of it was the blood of Henry Stoner.

As soon as he recovered from a head wound, which had permanently destroyed the hearing in his right ear, Nick was sent to Rhode Island, where his brother and father were stationed. But the joy of their reunion was marred when Henry Stoner was hit by a musket ball which embedded itself in his skull.

The surgeon said there was no hope—that Henry could not survive an operation. Knowing that his father would die anyway if the musket ball was not removed, Nick insisted that the surgeon at least try. The young man's desperate gamble paid off. His father eventually recovered, though he wore a silver plate in his skull until the day he died.

It was this silver plate that was to play an important part in Nick's later life, when he was given the reputation of being a vicious Indian-fighter.

The truth was something else. Nick's respect for Indians had not lessened during the years he had lived in the Mohawk Valley. If anything, it had grown as he learned more about their ways, especially those tribes which made up the vast Iroquois Confederation of the Six Nations: the Mohawks, Oneidas, Onondagas, Cayugas, Senecas and Tuscaroras.

Not only did Nick admire their expert woodsmanship and knowledge of medicine, but he was in sympathy with their respect for the land. The Indian lived in harmony with his environment, taking only what was necessary. This could not be said of the white man, who was already stripping the vast forests and killing off the abundant wildlife—often for no other reason than the sheer love of killing.

In addition, Nick felt that the Iroquois government—a democracy in which women held an equal place with men—was in some ways superior to that of his own. Because of these beliefs, Nicholas Stoner could never be regarded as an enemy of the red man.

On the other hand, Nick was well aware that not all Indians were friendly, especially when the Revolutionary War caused a split in the Iroquois Confederation. At that time, the Tuscaroras and Oneidas sided with the Americans, while the other four nations were sympathetic to the British, and former friends suddenly became enemies.

Henry Stoner became one of the many casualties. Having survived the surgeon's knife, he was discharged from the army one summer in time to reach home and

help with the crops. It was while he was hoeing in his corn-
field that a party of Canadian Indians attacked and
scalped him. They even took the piece of silver that had
been used to plug the hole in his skull where the musket
ball had penetrated.

When the news reached his son, then on duty at
King's Ferry, Nick vowed revenge. First, though, there
was a war to be won.

Before the Revolution was over, Nick was to wit-
ness all the many horrors of war—from the bloated corp-
ses littering the field at the Battle of Oriskany to Benedict
Arnold's bloody attack of the Hessian camp at Saratoga's
Bemis Heights. Because he had fought under Arnold and
knew of his bravery, Nick was more shocked than most
when the general turned traitor. Ironically, in September
1780, Nick was the fifer in the guard which escorted Major
John André—Benedict Arnold's British contact—to the
gallows.

Nick had also seen the horror of prison life, when
he was captured by the British and spent six months in the
notorious pest-hole on Conanicut Island near Rhode
Island. Therefore, when peace was finally declared in
1783, Nick headed back to his beloved Mohawk Valley,
hoping that he would never again have to pick up a musket
for any reason other than hunting.

Such a hope was unrealistic in the still untamed
Adirondack country, and Nick had not been home for
very long when he was called upon to act as deputy sheriff
—a duty which would add to the growing legend about
him.

It was while Nick was still deputy sheriff that the
final incident of his father's silver plate occurred. There
had been trouble at the local public house, and when Nick
arrived he saw a strange Indian showing off his scalping
knife to some friends inside. Indicating nine notches, the
Indian boasted of taking the scalps of nine white men, including that of "Old Stoner."

That was all Nick had to hear. Picking up the
nearest weapon he could find—in this case, an andiron

from the fireplace — he flattened the Indian with one fierce blow. Before he could continue his attack, the wounded Indian's companions had come to his rescue and took him out of there.

No one can say what might have happened had they not acted so quickly. For right after they left, Nick Stoner discovered something that the Indian had dropped when he struck him — it was the silver plate from Henry Stoner's skull!

Life was not always that violent, however, and Nick Stoner spent much of his time hunting and fishing in the woods, as well as trapping in the wintertime. In later years he also became a well-known guide. He was so successful at all these pursuits that even today when stories are told around an Adirondack campfire, his name is often the first one mentioned.

During his wilderness treks, Nick usually traveled a particular route which came to be called the Nick Stoner Trail. There were occasions, though, when he abandoned his regular paths and traveled as far north as the St. Lawrence Valley.

It was on one of these excursions that Nick found himself the hunted rather than the hunter. For some reason now lost in the mists of time, a party of Indians began tracking him as he skirted Cranberry Lake in what is now St. Lawrence County. Unable to outdistance his pursuers, Nick hid in a nearby rock shelter until he could proceed on his way unmolested.

This shelter, now known as Stoner's Cave, was formed by the tip of one massive boulder being tilted into position on top of another by glacial action. Because of its unusual configuration, the cave became a favorite spot for hikers in the area. They still enjoy its welcome shelter just as Nick Stoner did more than a century ago.

STONER'S CAVE

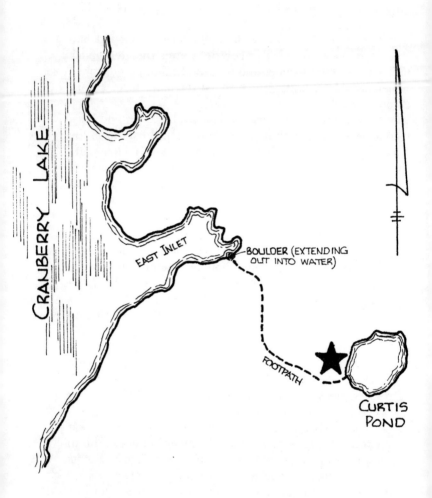

CRANBERRY LAKE

EAST INLET

BOULDER (EXTENDING OUT INTO WATER)

FOOTPATH

CURTIS POND

How to Get There

Stoner's Cave, near the village of Cranberry Lake, New York. The easiest way to get to Stoner's Cave is to take a boat from the village of Cranberry Lake (or from the public campsite south of the village, off Lone Pine Road) to the East Inlet of Cranberry Lake. At the eastern tip of the inlet, you will see a large boulder which extends out into the water from the shoreline. Almost directly in back of this boulder can be found the start of a trail marked by the New York State Department of Environmental Conservation. (The markers are red discs with white lettering around the edges, and are placed on trees at convenient intervals.) Follow this trail through the marshy area bordering the lake, then up the slopes (a stiff climb) for about half a mile. At this point the trail gradually descends to Curtis Pond, which is approximately another half mile away. The cave is next to the trail, about 150 feet from the edge of Curtis Pond. (Approximate walking time: 30 minutes from the start of the trail at the East Inlet of Cranberry Lake.)

16 Clues To Caving

When to Go

Whenever you are looking for a cave in unfamiliar territory, it is usually best to go in the late fall or early spring. At such times the foliage is not thick and it is easier to spot the cave, as well as landmarks and trail signs. Needless to say, the lack of foliage also helps to prevent you from getting lost should you stray off the trail or become confused.

Late fall and early spring are also good caving times because the weather is cooler—a decided advantage in view of the fact that the route to most caves lies uphill.

During such seasons you are less likely to encounter snakes. This is something that must be kept in mind, as New York State has two poisonous varieties: copperheads and timber rattlers.

Actually the danger of getting bitten by a snake is much less than most people imagine. Given half a chance, a snake will rather run than bite. (For all the many caves described in this book—some of them visited on more than one occasion—the author encountered a snake only once. Moreover, that one was at least fifteen feet away and down the inaccessible face of a cliff.) So with the following "snake sense" rules, you should have no trouble at all:

●Stay on the trail.

•Never place your hand or foot in a place you cannot see. (For instance, never step *over* a fallen tree. First step *on* it, glance at what is on the other side, then step down. This is a good rule for avoiding sprained ankles, as well.)

•If you see a snake, leave it alone. Don't try to push it, poke it out of the way, or try to kill it. Just walk around it, giving it a wide berth. Above all, don't decide to take a baby snake home as a pet. Not only is most wildlife (and that includes snakes) protected by law in public parks, but a baby snake of the poisonous variety is just as dangerous as a full-grown one.

How to Go

If you are an inexperienced hiker or in unfamiliar territory, always stay on the trail or path you are supposed to follow. Don't take shortcuts even if you are positive that such a shortcut would be better — usually it isn't.

Remember that directions are always given *to* a place, and you must reverse them on the way back. An uphill path will become a downhill one. A landmark which appeared on your left going up will be on your right going back, and it may not even look the same when viewed from a different angle.

Never rush. If you don't have time to make the trip at a comfortable and safe pace, then save the trip until another time when you do. This is especially true when climbing over rocks. Many a hiker has taken a nasty fall only because he was in a rush.

Be careful of moss-covered rocks. They are slippery. Don't even step on them if you can avoid it. Test the stability of a rock before putting all your weight on it — a shifting rock has caused more than one skinned knee or worse.

As for handholds when climbing rocks, make certain they are firm before trusting them. Never grab hold of a dead or fallen tree limb or trunk; no matter how stout they may look, chances are that they aren't. If you need to take hold of something, a live and firmly rooted shrub such as green mountain laurel is usually the best bet.

Remember that fallen leaves may mask an uneven surface or a hole in the ground. Some hikers carry walking sticks (any fairly straight, fallen tree branch can be picked up along the trail) to test such areas. However, many experienced hikers prefer to leave both hands free.

Who to Go With

Never go hiking or cave exploring alone, and always be sure someone at home (or a park ranger) knows where you or your group are heading. Although the caves mentioned in this book are, for the most part, in well-traveled areas and not difficult to locate, there is always the possibility of some accident or getting lost.

If, by some mischance, you do become confused and cannot find the correct trail within a few minutes, sit down and wait. *Do not keep walking.* That only makes it more difficult to find you. Stay in one place.

What to Take With You

A compass and map are musts whenever you are heading for one of the more remote caves. Carry your own and don't depend on the other fellow to have them. If you are following verbal directions rather than a map, be sure to write them down and keep them in your pocket for easy reference. Don't depend on your memory.

Be sure to carry a canteen of water, as uphill treks always produce thirst, and you should never drink from any stream or river, no matter how pure the water may appear.

If you plan to eat on the trail or at the cave, pack food that is lightweight and easy to carry. (In the summer, be certain your food is of the nonperishable kind.) Many hikers make it a rule to always have a quick-energy snack, such as a candy bar, in their pocket.

Remember that even the smallest cave can be

mighty dark when only a few feet inside. Therefore, a flashlight or candles should be part of your pack. In larger caves, you should *always* have at least three independent sources of light.

It is also good sense to carry along a small first-aid kit as well as a snakebite kit. You may never have reason to use them, but if the need arises, you will be glad they are available.

Most first-aid kits do not include one, but a bar of soap is a good addition in the event that you come in contact with poison ivy, which occurs everywhere. Though this three-leafed menace is most potent during the summertime, when the leaves are soft, do not take any chance with it in the cooler months either. If you do come in contact with it, immediate and careful washing (lathering and rinsing at least three times) may well prevent weeks of later discomfort.

One last thing for your pack should be a small can or bottle of insect repellent. This should be used liberally on hair and clothing, as well as exposed surfaces of the skin.

These are the basic necessities for comfortable and safe cave-hunting, all of which can be carried in a small pack on your back or at your side, leaving your hands free. Above all, don't load yourself up with unnecessary equipment—a hill becomes progressively steeper for every extra pound you carry.

As for clothing, hiking attire may be anything comfortable and suitable to the weather. Shoes should have nonslip soles and be sturdy enough to provide adequate support. Long pants are preferred rather than shorts or a skirt because they are good protection against insects, poison ivy and scratches from underbrush or rocks.

How to be a Responsible Caver

There are only a few simple rules that are followed by thoughtful hikers and cavers to preserve the places they visit for the enjoyment of others.

•Always take out what you carry in. If everyone did that, there would be no problem of litter.

•If you start a fire, make sure it is out before you leave. Use only dead wood, which usually is easy to find in any forest area, rather than injuring a live tree. If there are "No Campfires Allowed" signs around, heed them. They were put there for a good reason.

•If you will be going across private land, try to secure the owner's permission beforehand. Make sure you leave everything as you found it—especially gates in fences. If you find a gate closed, make sure it is that way after you go through it.

•In these days of graffiti, it is hard to find a place not marred by someone's spray paint, but you should not add to the defacing of natural beauty. If you want to leave a record of your visit, you can always set up a small stone cairn (rock pile) with a note inside.

•Digging for artifacts such as arrowheads is against the law in practically all places. It is allowed only when a permit has been issued by the proper authorities. Amateurs have ruined many a fine archeological site, so don't bring a trowel along unless you are a member of a group which has a permit to dig.

By following these rules of responsible caving, you will help to preserve our wilderness and historic areas for the countless others who will follow in your footsteps—a precious gift which only you can bestow.

Acknowledgments

One of the most enjoyable things about writing a book like this is the many fine people you meet, either in person or through letters. Although it is not possible to name each and every person who contributed his time and interest to the preparation of *Caves For Kids,* the following people were especially helpful:

Walter Averill, Hudson River Valley Association; Dan Bednarski, Niagara Frontier State Park Commission; Tom Boyce, Dover Plains National Bank; Gary Buckingham Sr.; Gary Buckingham Jr.; C.V. Crane and Cornelius Cuddeback, Minisink Valley Historical Society; Arthur Detmers, Buffalo and Erie County Historical Society; and Arthur Einhorn, Lewis County Historian.

Also: Mrs. Charles Franklin, Putnam County Historical Society; Mrs. Hugh Kelley; Jack Krajewski, Niagara Frontier State Park Commission; Donald E. Loker, Niagara Falls Public Library; Jay and Sue McMahon; Arthur Nordby, Fillmore Glen State Park; Donald F. Oliver, Finger Lakes State Parks and Recreation Commission; and Raymond Pearson, Lake George Institute of History, Art and Science.

In addition: Clarence A. Petty, Adirondack Park Agency; Nial T. Phelps, Historian of the town of Diana; Mrs. Wilhelmina B. Powers, Adriance Memorial Library; Fred F. Reeve; Mrs. J. E. Saffron, Port Jervis Chamber of Commerce; Nicholas Shoumatoff, Ward Pound Ridge Reservation; Philip G. Terrie Jr., Adirondack Museum; Beverly and Dick Titus; Gary K. Walrath, Glens Falls Historical Association; Gardner F. Watts, Village of Suffern Historian; Ruth N. Wilcox, Library of the Museum of the American Indian; and Marjorie F. Williams, City Historian of Niagara Falls.

My thanks are also offered to Douglas L. Turner of the Buffalo *Courier-Express* for permission to use the picture of Devil's Hole Cave; and to Judson D. Hale at *Yankee* for allowing me to reprint parts of my article on the Old Leatherman.

Sources

Some of *New York's Caves for Kids* is based on legends and oral traditions related to me by local historians and others, whose names can be found in the Acknowledgments section. Considerable material was also found by digging through old newspapers. For basic research, I relied on such books as Clay Perry's *Underground Empire* (1948); *A History of New York State,* compiled by D. M. Eliss, J.A. Frost, H.C. Syrett and H.F. Carman (1967); *New York Walk Book,* compiled by the New York-New Jersey Trail Conference and the American Geographical Society (1971); *New York: A Guide to the Empire State,* compiled by the WPA Writers' Program (1940); the *Dictionary of American Biography,* edited by Allen Johnson (1928); and *Notable American Women,* edited by E.T. James (1971). Other printed sources for individual chapters are as follows:

1. THE INDIANS OF INWOOD. *History of the City of New York,* by D.T. Valentine (1853); *Memorial History of the City of New-York,* by J.G. Wilson (1892); *Narratives of New Netherland,* edited by J.F. Jameson (1909); *The Forests and Wetlands of New York City,* by Elizabeth Barlow (1969); and *Indian Life of Long Ago in the City of New York,* by R.P. Bolton (1934, reprinted 1972).

2. HAVEN FOR ANNE HUTCHINSON. Some of the sources given for "Lairs of the Leatherman" also contain references to Helicker's Cave. In addition, Clark Wissler's *The Indians of Greater New York and the Lower Hudson* (1909) was consulted, as well as *Westchester County and Its People,* by E.F. Griffin (1946); and *The History of Westchester County,* by Frederic Shonnard and W.W. Spooner (1900).

3. LAIRS OF THE LEATHERMAN. It would be impossible to record here the many sources used for the story of the Old Leatherman, as I have for several years been collecting the numerous accounts concerning him that have appeared in both national and local periodicals. There is one article, however, that is basic to any research on the Old Leatherman. It is Allison Albee's three-part study, "The Leather Man," which appeared in the *Bulletin of the Westchester County Historical Society* for April, July and October 1937. Connecticut caving expert Leroy Foote's chapter in *Celebrated American Caves,* edited by C.E. Mohr and H.N. Sloane (1955), is of particular merit, as is his article in the *Bulletin of the National Speleological Society* for December 1956. A briefer account can be found in *Depths of the Earth,* by W.R. Halliday (1966), while in 1977 F.M. Johnson brought out a volume entitled *The Romantic Legend of Jules Bourglay.*

4. COUNTERFEITER'S "FACTORY." The history of the "Money Hole" is given in detail in Volume C of the *Nelson Scrapbook* (1880's) owned by the Putnam County Historical Society in Cold Spring.

5. HOME FOR A HERMITESS. Scharf's *History of Westchester County* (1886) recounts the story of Sarah Bishop, as does *When Our Town Was Young,* written by students of the North Salem Central High School (1945).

6. SASSACUS FINDS A REFUGE. *Historic Dover,* by R.F. Maher (1908); and *Handbook of American Indians North of Mexico,* by F. Hodge (1912).

7. THE DENS OF CLAUDIUS SMITH. One of the most notorious "cowboys" of the Revolutionary period, the story of Claudius Smith is accessible in such works as Quinlan's *History of Sullivan County* (1873); *History of Orange County, New York,* by E.M. Ruttenber and L.H. Clark (1881); *The Revolutionary War in the Hackensack Valley,* by A.C. Leiby (1962); *Tales and Towns of Northern New Jersey,* by H.C. Beck (1964); *Legends of the Shawangunk,* by P.H. Smith (1965); and "The Legend of Claudius Smith," by G.F. Watts (#4 in the "Discover Rockland" series of brochures put out by the Cooperative Extension of Cornell University, 1968).

8. ICEBOX FOR A NATURALIST. Based, in part, on an interview with Elizabeth Burroughs Kelley, who kindly gave permission for the quotes I use from her grandfather John Burroughs' books, *Time and Change* (1912), and *Under the Apple-Trees* (1916). Burroughs' description of the Boreas River cave can be found in *Wake-Robin* (1871), while his first ascent of Slide Mountain is detailed in Mrs. Kelley's *With John Burroughs in Field and Wood* (1969).

9. A GIFT FROM THE ENEMY. *Hudson River Landings,* Paul Wilstach (1933); *The Bicentennial Guide to the American Revolution,* by Sol Stemper (1974); *Revolutionary War Times in Highland Area and Ulster County,* compiled by B.W. Wadlin (1976); and "Highland and New Paltz" in *Hudson Valley* magazine (November 1975).

10. REAL CAVES IN FICTION. *The Pioneers,* by J.F. Cooper (1823); *Cooperstown,* by L.C. Jones (1949); *New York in Literature,* by R.R. and O.E. Wilson (1947); and *New York State Yesterday and Today,* by M.A. Wheeler (1952).

11. NIAGARA'S PIT OF THE EVIL SPIRIT. *Niagara County, New York,* by E.T. Williams (1921); *Visitors Guide to Niagara Falls,* by D.E. Loker (1969); and *A Brief History of Niagara Falls, New York,* by M.F. Williams (1972).

12. STRANGE PARTNERSHIP—THE VENGEANCE OF TOM QUICK AND CAHOONZIE. Tom Quick is another of New York's folk heroes whose name is frequently seen in books dealing with the state's history. Some of them are: *Hawk's Nest, or the Last of the Cahoonshees,* by J.M. Allerton (n.d.); *Legends of the Shawangunk,* by P.H. Smith (1965); *The Old Mine Road,* by C.G. Hine (1909, reprinted 1963); and J.E. Quinlan's *The Original Life and Adventures of Tom Quick, the Indian Slayer* (1894).

13. WHERE MILLARD FILLMORE ROAMED. *Millard Fillmore,* by R.J. Rayback (1959); *A Finger Lakes Odyssey,* by Lois O'Connor (1975); and *The Finger Lakes State Parks,* compiled by the Finger Lakes State Parks Commission (1972).

14. ESCAPE FROM ALPINA. I.M. Priest's *The Why of Lake Bonaparte and Natural Bridge, New York* (1938), and *Continued History of Lake Bonaparte, New York* (#2, 1939 and #3, 1940); *Adirondack Country,* by W.C. White (1967); *Tales from the Adirondack Foothills,* by Howard Thomas (1971); and *Historical Sketches of Northern New York and the Adirondack Wilderness,* by N.B. Sylvester (1877, reprinted 1973).

15. NORTH COUNTRY HIDEOUT. *Trappers of New York,* by J.R. Simms (1851); *Nicholas Stoner or a Tale of the Adirondacks,* by D.R. Williams (1969); and *New York State Folktales, Legends and Ballads,* by H.W. Thompson (originally published as *Body, Boots and Britches* in 1939, reprinted 1962).